COMMONALITIES IN PSYCHOSOMATIC MEDICINE

COMMONALITIES IN PSYCHOSOMATIC MEDICINE

By

HAROLD GEIST, Ph. D.

WARREN H. GREEN, INC.
St. Louis, Missouri, U.S.A.

Published by

WARREN H. GREEN, INC.
8356 Olive Boulevard
St. Louis, Missouri 63132, U.S.A.

ISBN No. 87527-485-4

Printed in the United States of America

FOREWORD

Over the past century, the advances of medical science have made possible the virtual eradication of infectious diseases, and have contributed greatly to the understanding and management of many types of illnesses. Those diseases most in need of study fall under the heading of psychophysiological or more popularly, psychosomatic diseases. Doctor Geist has pioneered in putting together common elements in a number of psychosomatic conditions. These studies greatly enhance the understanding and treatment not only of those diseases described, but also the many other psychosomatic ailments.

Arthur E. Gladman, M.D., F.A.P.A. (Life)
President, Telecare Corporation
Gladman Memorial Hospital,
Clinic and Psychosomatic Center
Oakland, California

ACKNOWLEDGMENTS

I would like to thank Ms. Glenna Goulet for patiently typing the manuscript, Doctor Sandra Whitaker for giving me moral support during the writing of the manuscript and finally to the publisher, Warren Green, who competently published two other books of mine.

Harold Geist

TABLE OF CONTENTS

COMMONALITIES IN PSYCHOSOMATIC MEDICINE

CHAPTER 1

Psychosomatic medicine has been sort of the Cinderella sister of medicine and stepchild of clinical psychology and psychiatry. The dichomotous fallacies based on Cartesian dualism is gradually being merged into a healthy child or a holistic approach to a sick individual. However, in the large rubric of these diseases, we still do not know the causes or treatment. For example, we are still in the experimental stages in getting at the definitive etiology of many diseases we label psychosomatic. I have devoted 15 years to the experimental study of five so called "psychosomatic diseases" and thought it time to combine the knowledge gained from this psychological research, both commonalities and differences, and see if there is a common thread of sameness and differences so that practitioners can add to the armentarium of weapons in combatting these conditions. Those of you who have read my books and articles on idiopathic epilepsy, rheumatoid arthritis, dermatoses, heart disease and migraine will realize that research on these and similar conditions is never ending. However, there comes a time when a compendium should be achieved and then start new and fresh areas of fertile soil to see if any further human suffering can be ameliorated.

Throughout my studies, I have consistently tried to deal with diseased people rather than diseased organs. In the inevitable comparisons and contrasts of the various psychosomatic conditions that one will talk of "states," "areas," "organs," etc. but it should be remembered that we have but one body and mind. Let us see if we can find more about this and these various conditions.

EPILEPSY

The modern period of the conception of epilepsy may be dated from the thesis of Bravais presented for the degree of M.D. at the University of Paris, in which he described localized forms of epilepsy which seemed to have a more favorable prognosis than generalized forms. In the middle of the 19th century, physiologists like Fritsch and Hitzig (2) and clinicians like Gowers studied the neurological pathways involved in the seizures, and found a drug which had definite value in the control of convulsive seizures. However, it was not until Jackson that the facts of epilepsy became well known, and although he propounded many erroneous hypotheses, his theories included the facts which guide most of our present-day thinking about epilepsy and cerebral localization. It was not, however, until the experimental demonstration of the electrical excitability of the cerebral cortex, in 1870 by Fritsch and Hitzig and in 1873 by Ferrier, that Jackson's ideas began to receive general acceptance. In 1881, the first edition of a monumental clinical approach to the subject was published. The modern period of investigation and research may be dated from 1920, when an osteopathic practitioner advertised the fact that complete abstinence tended to hold seizures in abeyance. Following these observations, there have been modern studies in chemistry and electroencephalography.

INCIDENCE

The incidence of epilepsy has been calculated at more than one percent of the total population in the United States. It is greater among children than adults, and there does not seem to be any sex difference.

Based on the incidence of epilepsy in Rochester, Minnesota, the estimated current prevalence in the U.S. is 522,000–757,000 (Kurland, J. *Chronic Dis* (1958), 378). The risk of having a "cryptogenic epileptic" child is increased in older primipera (Herloft, Leinal, and Semonsen, *Acta Psychiat Neurol Scand* 33 (1958), 296). There is a high correlation with breech deliveries.

TYPES

CLINICAL CLASSIFICATION

The classification of epilepsy is difficult and is disputed today even among authorities on the subject. It is customary among present-day writers to speak of epilepsies produced by a discoverable disease process as symptomatic and those not due to some organic brain disease or abnormal somatic condition as idiopathic or genuine epilepsy. This latter group includes those of unknown cause and has also come to refer to those which are merely excluded from the symptomatic.

CLASSIFICATION ACCORDING TO SEIZURES

Wilson has proposed a classification of the epilepsies as follows:

1. Motor Epilepsy
   a. Myoclonic jerks without loss of consciousness
   b. Epilepsia partialis continuosa (Kojewnikow's epilepsy)
   c. Tonic epilepsy (so-called cerebellar fits)
   d. Coordinated epilepsy (grand mal)
   e. Akinetic epilepsy (transient flaccid states)
2. Sensory Epilepsy
   a. Reflex

b. Sensory
c. Affective
3. Psychic Variants
4. Visceral Variants
5. Focal Epilepsy

This classification includes the main clinical types. Also to be included is the classification according to the attacks or seizures, depending upon their severity. Thus there is the major *grand mal,* a severe attack, and the minor *petit mal,* a slight attack.

Penfield has attempted a classification according to clinical types and localization in the brain.

In general, however, the classification of the epilepsies is, at best, in a confused state. Grinker has suggested speaking of the epilepsies as "convulsive states." In the "Diagnostic and Statistical Manual of Mental Disorders" of the American Psychiatric Association, the term epilepsy no longer denotes a disease entity; it is used as a symptom of convulsive disorders.

The terms idiopathic, genuine, and essential epilepsy have been followed primarily in this country because of the work of Lennox. Alstrom, in his comprehensive study in Sweden, has suggested discarding the old terms. He "considered it more correct to classify the material into epilepsy of unknown, probably, and known etiology." It is this classification which appears most suitable to the writer.

SYMPTOMOLOGY

1. Prodromal symptoms frequently precede the major attacks or manifest themselves before a series of motor attacks. Their significance is unknown, but they are suggestive of some general or local metabolic disturbance which is accumulating in quantity. They are manifest several days or often only a few hours before the attack.
2. Paroxysmal prodromata may occur in the form of brief dreamy states or temporary subjective feelings of strangeness. They may be sudden myoclonic jerks affecting groups of muscles in one or all extremities. There also my be dysesthesias or "pins," "needles," and sudden momentary abdominal pain, choking, hiccoughs, or palpitation of the heart.
3. Continuous prodromata may appear for a day or two preceding an attack, in the form of increased irritability or lethargy. By various indescribable actions or changes in disposition, the patient shows evidence of an impending attack. There is usually a

appetite, generalized headache, or pallor. Some people become euphoric or ecstatic preceding an attack.

The aura which immediately precedes or initiates the convulsion consists usually of a sensation of dizziness, of discomfort in the abdomen, or in special cases, a tingling in an extremity. A *grand mal* attack is preceded, in about half of all patients, by a premonitory symptom. Grinker describes various types of auras. Some auras (about 20 percent of the cases with warnings, including the idiopathic type) are localized in an arm, leg, one side of the face, as peculiar sensations in the throat, breathlessness, nausea, choking, palpitation, vertigo, and peculiar head feelings. Psychic auras are feelings of horror or fright. Cursive epilepsy is an example of such fear preceding an attack. Here the patient runs from his initial position crying out some manifestation of horror, until he falls unconscious.

The attacks themselves may be described as the *grand mal,* Jacksonian, *petit mal,* or psychic equivalent seizures.

In the *grand mal* seizure, the patient loses consciousness, the muscles become rigid, respiration is suspended, and he falls if not supported. Because of the suspended respiration, the face becomes pallid, the color clearing only with the return of air to the lungs, which occurs when movements, instead of being rigid (tonic), become jerking (clonic). A severe convulsion may be preceded by headache, vomiting, muscular soreness, and depression. Sometimes attacks succeed one another without the patient gaining consciousness; this is *status epilepticus.*

A special type of *grand mal* convulsion begins in an extremity and spreads toward the brain; the patient retains consciousness but is unable to stop the spasmodic movements. Jacksonian seizures, when present, point to the corresponding area of the brain, the cells of which are discharging abnormally.

In the *petit mal* attack, the predominant feature is the loss of consciousness. Usually unconsciousness begins and ends abruptly. Sometimes it is not complete and the attack consists more of twitching motions of the muscles about the eye, which recur with regular frequency, often many times a day.

In the psychic equivalent seizures (psychic variants, psychomotor seizures), the predominant symptom is amnesia. The patient may perform purposeful acts but cannot remember what he did. These seizures are longer than *petit mal,* lasting from a fraction of a minute to hours or even, sometimes, days. However, Boschi states that the lack of mnemonic fixation does not necessarily mean unconsciousness during an epileptic attack. The recall of a criminal act does not exclude the epileptic and ego, in certain cases, facilitate the persistence of consciousness. The muscular movements are clonic.

According to Lennox, nearly one half of the patients have more than one type. Half the patients have only *grand mal,* 8 percent have *petit mal,* and 1 percent psychic seizures. "With or without another type of seizure, grand mal occurs in 90 percent of patients, *petit mal* in 45 percent, and psychic in 8 percent."

METHODS OF MEDICAL DIAGNOSIS

SEIZURES

The initial method of diagnosing epilepsy is by observing the seizures. Major attacks are often preceded by the epileptic cry. It is a violent screaming sound produced by spasm of the thoracic and abdominal muscles expelling air through the glottis. The cry apparently occurs just at the time of loss of consciousness. This is followed by spasm of the limbs, remission to clonic spasm, and is accompanied by foaming at the mouth and, frequently, biting of the tongue and cheek. During the major attacks, the pupils are usually dilated and rarely react to light. After an attack, the patient may pass directly into a heavy sleep or may awaken from unconsciousness for a brief period and then lapse into a deep sleep. A weakness in one arm or leg (Todd's post-epileptic paralysis) may last for a few days after the attack and then gradually recede, even when there is no organic disease. There are other varieties of major attacks which do not particularly concern this study.

Minor attacks are variable in nature and take the form of giddiness, feeling of strangeness, dreamy sensations, and sudden sensory phenomena related to visual, auditory or gustatory areas. These will be discussed in more detail in examining the unknown group in this study.

ELECTROENCEPHALOGRAM

One of the primary methods of diagnosing epilepsy is by means of electroencephalogram.* The first attempt at this was made by Berger, who made electroencephalographic records of patients at the time they were having seizures. Davies showed additional features, viz., that an approximately three-per-second alteration between a spike and a slow wave occurs with *petit mal* seizures; pure fast discharge occurs with the tonic phase, tonic-clonic, or *grand mal* seizures, and a flat-topped four-per-second wave mixed with high voltage six-per-second waves occurs in psychic seizures, psychic equivalents, or psychomotor seizures. Very slow waves occur with ordinary post-seizure stupor.

Gibbs, Davis, and Lennox discovered that abnormalities might be present when patients were not displaying any symptoms. *Petit mal*

---

*See page 108, appendix for electroencephalogram of four cases.

patients might show disturbances of rhythm which were in reality very short of low voltage seizure discharges. Later it was found that about 85 percent of patients with a history of seizures showed abnormalities of rhythm in an inter-paroxysmal period, during a twenty-minute period of observation.

About 10 percent of normal persons exhibit abnormalities which are similar to those encountered in patients who have a history of seizures or related conditions. According to Lennox, these persons might be called asymptomatic potential epileptics. Such conditions are not peculiar. Many persons who have no cardiac symptoms can be shown, by laboratory methods, to have disturbances in the rhythm of the heart. Many persons who are not diabetic have a high blood sugar curve. Individuals with asymptomatic dysrhythmia outnumber those with seizures approximately twenty to one. Presumably, they form the reservoir out of which persons with symptoms are recruited.

These abnormal potentials are encountered in conditions other than epilepsy. They are common in all conditions where seizures are common; for example, in feeble-minded children and families of epileptics, in paresis, in meningovascular syphilis, and in brain tumor. Although they occur in association with seizures, they occur also in the absence of seizures which are clinically observable.

As stated previously, the clinical terms *petit mal* and *grand mal* are usually used to refer to seizure patterns. Gibbs and Gibbs speak in terms of "electrical activity" because of the vagueness of the clinical concepts. "The clinical terminology would be simplified and improved if the term *petit mal* were restricted to conditions in which a three-second wave and spike discharge is present or is presumed to be present; similarly, *grand mal* and psychomotor seizures."

Seizure discharges which are unaccompanied by clinical evidence of a seizure are called subclinical seizures. They are common in persons with *petit mal,* less common in psychomotor disorders, and rare in those with *grand mal*. Discharges of short duration are called larval seizures; for example a single wave and spike formulation and a very short *grand mal* or a psychomotor discharge lasting a fraction of a second. Yakovlev and Hodskins state that, clinically, epilepsy is a condition characterized by a defective regulation of the rate at which energy is released by the central nervous system. Gibbs called it a "cerebral dysrhythmia."

Neurologists will argue that epilepsy, no matter what form has an organic cause. However, I will cling to the functional viewpoint that there is one type of epilepsy known as idiopathic, where the origin or cause is unknown, and will continue to be. Certainly, the dynamics of idiopathic epilepsy are quite different from the organic.* In my research on idiopathic epileptics, I used 7 different kinds of tests each contributing to the dynamics of idiopathic epileptics. There is certainly a hysterical component to this and symbolic indications of hostile periodic outbursts, controlled at times, and directed at male figures. There also seems to be a disturbed oedipal situation with almost universal dislike of father figures, and frequent sexually toned dreams, accompanied by an unsatisfactory sex life. There are also obsessive compulsive tendencies and psychopathic traits. Disregard for current mores and restricted ability to express deep emotional responses and immaturity are coupled with intense conflict, resulting from an unsatisfactory sexual adjustment. What happens with idiopathic epileptics is the obsessive compulsive defenses hold these patients together and at times the "trigger" is fired and a fit ensues. Tensions overpower idiopathic epileptics to such a degree that they have difficulty in solving every day problems. These epileptics have what may be termed a "burnt child" constellation with toned down overt reactions to others for fear of being "wounded." The Rorschachs can best be summarized by the term "defensive regression," a regression to an earlier stage of psychosexual development caused by a super ego colliding head on with unacceptable anal references, and this may be the immediate cause of the convulsion. The TATs indicate aggressive tendencies toward father figures. In other projective tests the father is seen as a castrating and censuring agent and it may be in this relationship that we have the primary clue to the hysterical nature of the convulsion. The obsessive compulsive hysterical nature of these patients is reiterated in their drawings. Let us talk more fully what happens in idiopathic epilepsy.

THEORETICAL SPECULATIONS

I believe that in order to understand what happens in the unknown type of epilepsy, we must go back to the speculations of Penfield and Jasper. Penfield believes that epileptic seizures begin as an abnormal discharge in the centroencephalic nervous system (pons, midbrain, and basal diencephalon) which radiates to the homologous areas of the two hemispheres. In the *petit mal* seizure, the participation of the cortex is a more or less passive one; in the *grand mal* seizure, there is a greater intensity and bombardment of the cortex. This is the mechanism of the

*Geist, H. Etiology of Idiopathic Epilepsy. Exposition Press, Smithtown, N.Y., 1962.

seizure, whether it is due to organic or other reasons. Psychical hallucinatory seizures which resemble true dreams have been reproduced artificially by Penfield, in the temporal lobe and the posterior parietal cortex adjacent to it. Dreams result from abnormalities in the memory cortex, where ictal discharges activate selected ganglionic patterns. The discharge can pass from one anatomical area to the other, producing various other kinds of psychical phenomena. In the case of a tumor or physical trauma, there is no problem. The *agent provocateur* of the convulsion initiates the discharge in the sub-cortical structures whence it is projected into the cortex. But what of those cases where there is no organic provocation? For this answer, we must go to the speculations of Freud and Breuer on hysteria and compare them with the experimental evidence we have obtained.

Breuer, in his theoretical speculations concerning hysteria (Freud and Breuer, *Studies of Hysteria*), speaks of the difference between a clear waking state and dreamless sleep. Breuer says, "We shall perhaps only be describing these facts in other words if we say that in sleep the paths of connection and conduction in the brain are not traversable by excitations of the psychical elements (? cortical cells) whereas in waking life, they are completely so traversable. The existence of these two different conditions of the paths of conduction can, it seems, only be made intelligible if we suppose that in waking life those paths are in a state of tonic excitation (what Exner calls intercellular tetanus), that this cerebral excitation is what determines their conductive capability, and that diminution and disappearance of that excitation is what sets up the state of sleep."

During waking life, unpleasurable feelings corresponding to excitement cause an increase in normal intracerebral excitation, resulting in what Freud calls "unpleasurable." Likewise, during waking life, there is going on what Freud calls the principle of constancy of "neuronic inertia"—quite similar to Cannon's principle of homeostasis. These increases in indigenous excitation, according to both Freud and Breuer, are due to psychical affects initiated by sexual excitation and sexual affect. Such affects "level out" the increased excitation by motor discharges. In some instances, the affect can find no discharge of excitation of any kind, and we get what Oppenheim calls "an abnormal expression of emotions," of what Freud and Breuer call hysterical conversion. Breuer writes further: "The motor actions in which the excitation of affects is normally discharged are ordered and coordinated even though they are often useless. But an excessively strong excitation may bypass or break through the coordinative centers and flow off in primitive movements. In infants, apart from the respiratory action of screaming, affects only produce and find expression in uncoordinated contractions of the muscles of this primitive kind—in arching the body and kicking about. As development proceeds, the musculature passes more and more under the control of the power of coordination and the will.

"But the opisthotonous, which represents the maximum of motor effort of the total somatic musculature, and the clonic movements of kicking and thrashing about, persist throughout life as the form of reaction for the maximal excitation of the brain—for the purely physical excitation in epileptic attacks as well as for the discharge of maximal effects in the shape of more or less epileptoid convulsions (viz., the purely motor part of hysterical attacks)." (Freud and Breuer, pp. 204–5.)

In speaking of the dream process, Freud says, "The hallucinations of hysteria and paranoia, as well as the visions of mentally normal persons, I would explain as corresponding in fact to regressions, i.e., to thoughts transformed into images; and would assert that only such thoughts undergo this transformation as are in intimate connection with suppressed memories or with memories which have remained unconscious. I will, therefore, refer to my analysis of an hallucinatory paranoiac woman patient and to the results of my hitherto unpublished studies on the psychology of the psychoneuroses, in order to emphasize the fact that in these cases of regressive thought transformation, one must not overlook the influence of suppressed memories, or one that has remained unconscious, this usually being of an infantile character. This memory draws into regression, as it were, the thoughts with which it is connected and which are kept from expression by the censorship; that is, into that form of representation in which the memory itself is psychically existent. And here I may add, as a result of my studies on hysteria, that if one succeeds in bringing to consciousness infantile scenes (whether they are recollections or fantasies), they appear as hallucinations and are divested of this character only when they are communicated. It is known also that even in persons whose memories are not otherwise visual the earliest infantile memories remain vividly visual until late in life." (*Basic Writings of Sigmund Freud,* pp. 494–95.)

Certainly, defensive regression is a phenomenon characteristic of the unknown epileptics in this study. Freud speculates that in pathological regression, just as in dreams, the process of energy transference must be different from that occurring in the regressions of normal psychic life, since it renders possible a full hallucinatory cathexis of perception. But what causes this regression in the epileptic? It appears that it is the unacceptable sexual references, particularly in the Oedipal area, colliding with a well-developed superego. This probably takes place in the memory cortex, or there is a concomitant phenomenon in the subcortical areas radiating to the cortical lobes. Penfield has, indeed, artificially reproduced another regressive phenomenon in the memory cortex, viz., the dream. In the unknown epileptics in this study, one of the outstanding characteristics of the group is rebellion against father or father figures. The relation of Freud's conception of Dostoevski's epileptic attacks and the unknown group is quite clear now. The homosexual references make the position of the unknown epileptic all the more untenable.*

In speaking of hysterical attacks, Freud says, "When one psychoanalyses a patient subject to hysterical attacks, one soon gains the conviction that their attacks are nothing but fantasies projected and translated into motor activity and represented in pantomime. It is true that these fantasies are unconscious, but otherwise they are of the same nature as those that may be directly observed in daydreams or revealed by an interpretation of nocturnal dreams.

"An hysterical attack, therefore, must be subjected to the same analytic procedure as we use in dream interpretation. Not only are the forces producing the distortion and the purpose of this distortion the same as those we are familiar with from the interpretation of dreams, but the technique of the distortion is the same also." (Collected Papers, p. 46). He goes further: "The outbreak of hysterical attacks follows laws that are readily understood. Since the repressed complex consists of libidinal cathexis and ideational context (fantasy), the attack may be aroused (1) associatively if the content of the complex (sufficiently charged) is stirred by a conscious occurrence; (2) organically if from some internal somatic reasons or external influences on the mind the libidinal cathexis exceeds a certain amount." (*Collected Papers II,* 102.) The analogy between Freud's description and epilepsy is indeed striking. Freud claims that the loss of consciousness in hysteria is derived from the fleeting loss of consciousness observed at the climax of every intensive (and autoerotic) sexual gratification, and he has shown the unmistakable psychoanalytic implications of the unknown type of epilepsy.

The question arises as to why certain people are predisposed toward unknown epilepsy and others are not. Janet's explanation of predisposition to hysteria is "mental weakness" *(insuffisance psychologique).* The mental function of uniting ideas into a synthesis is low in hysterical patients. The excessive affectivity of these patients is accounted for by every idea taking possession of the whole of their limited mental activity.

---

*The fact that these epileptics had homosexual tendencies is not inconsistent with the fact they were immature and had mother fixations. Freud writes, "The first of these is that homosexual men have experienced a specially strong fixation."

"Hysteria, which is essentially based on this splitting of the mind, is a 'maladie par faiblesse' (disease due to weakness), and that is why it develops most readily when a mind which is innately weak is submitted to influences that weaken it still further or is faced by heavy demands in relation to which its weakness stands out still more." (Freud and Breuer, *Studies in Hysteria,* p. 231.)

Breuer, on the other hand, believes that the so-called weak-mindedness is due to a division of mental activity and that only part of the capacity is at the disposal of the hysteric's thoughts. He believes that what underlies hysterical dissociation is an "excess of efficiency, the habitual coexistence of two heterogeneous ideas." Breuer goes on: "I suspect that the duplication of psychical functioning, whether this is habitual or caused by emotional situations in life, acts as a substantial predisposition to genuine pathological splitting of the mind. This duplication passes over into the latter state if the content of the two co-existing sets of ideas is no longer of the same kind, if one of them contains ideas which are inadmissible to consciousness—which have been fended off, that is, or have arisen from hypnoid states. When this is so, it is impossible for the two temporarily divided streams to reunite, as is constantly happening in healthy people, and a region of unconscious psychical activity becomes permanently split off. This hysterical splitting of the mind stands in the same relation to the 'double ego' of a healthy person as does the hypnoid state to a normal reverie." (*Studies in Hysteria,* p. 234). Freud's observations and analyses show that the splitting of the mind can also be caused by "defence," "by the deliberate deflection of consciousness from distressing ideas; only however, in some people, to whom we must therefore ascribe a mental idiosyncracy." It makes no difference whether one adheres to the concepts of Janet or Breuer. In unknown epilepsy, the convulsion is due to the co-existence of two unacceptable trains of thought, one of which has become unacceptable to the harsh demands of the other.

PHYSICAL ASPECTS OF RHEUMATOID ARTHRITIS

Arthritis is one of the oldest diseases known to man. Bones of prehistoric men have shown that it was present in Neolithic cavemen and also in Egypt and Nubia in pre-dynastic natives. According to Rupfer, who introduced the word *paleopathology,* spondylitis deformens was very common among Egyptians, and evidence of the disease is present in Egyptian mummies dating to 8000 B.C. The word *rheumatism* was used by Dioscorides, Galen and Giullaume de Buillou to represent the supposed "defluxion of rheum" as a humour into a joint. Literally, in Greek, it means "to flow." Today rheumatic diseases are more prevalent than the total of cases of tuberculosis, diabetes, cancer and heart disease combined. It is estimated that in this country one in twenty people suffer from some form of rheumatism.

ETIOLOGY

The cause of rheumatoid arthritis is unknown. The infectious theory presupposes that infection with bacteria, protozoa or viruses plays an important role in the etiology of the disease. Most experts believe that many other factors may prepare the soil for infection—heredity, poor environment, accidental or some other type of trauma and dietary deficiencies are contributing causes of the disease. Some of the theories concerning the etiology of rheumatism are:

1. Focal infection;
2. Bacterial allergy;
3. Virus infection;
4. Vitamin deficiency;
5. Metabolic disorder;
6. Emotions involving psychopathology; and
7. Circulatory disturbance.

More recently, emotional aspects such as psychic shock and worry have been discovered to contribute to the disease.

Definite evidence concerning the possible infectious nature in rheumatoid arthritis is difficult to obtain. Cultures from blood, various foci of infection, the lymph nodes, stores, etc., have been analyzed in patients with rheumatoid arthritis with varying results. The findings which favor the infectious nature of rheumatoid arthritis are a leukocytosis, increased sedimentation rate, fever, inflammation of synovial membranes and periarticular tissue, exudative characteristics of the synovial fluid and enlarged lymph nodes.

Those who adhere to the infectious theory of arthritis claim the tubercle bacillus, gonococcus, hemolytic streptococcus and staphylococcus are the etiological agents in arthritis. Blood cultures in rheumatoid arthritis vary from completely negative to 69 per cent positive. In various studies approximately 50 to 90 per cent of patients with rheumatoid arthritis possess agglutinins to hemolytic streptococci, very often in high titer. More than 75 per cent of patients with rheumatoid arthritis show positive skin reactions to hemolytic streptococci. Those who argue that rheumatoid arthritis is solely an infectious disease should remember that many of the clinical features of rheumatoid arthritis are also exhibited by gouty arthritis, which is a metabolic disorder.

Rheumatoid arthritis occurs most usually in temperate climates, the incidence of the disease diminishing as we reach the equator; rheumatoid arthritis is almost unknown in the tropics. It seems to run in families, and usually more than one member of a family is affected; three quarters of the cases begin between ages twenty and fifty, with the zenith at about thirty-five years of age; females are more frequently affected than males in a ratio of about three to one, whites are more affected than Negroes. Other concomitant factors are poor home environment, trauma, both physical and mental, poverty and family ways. Arthritis has been found to be common to those who do cleaning work which requires spending a good deal of time with their hands in cold water.

Certain theories about the pathology of the anatomy around the affected organ has been postulated. For example, paraneuritic nodules have been found by Freund and Leichentritt. They are thought to be the result of a definite systemic disturbance. Other investigators have postulated that a spasm of the small peripheral veins may have some connection with the disease. Another theory is that rheumatoid arthritis may be due to a disorder of hyaluronic acid metabolism.* The arteriolar spasm results in the delivery of an enzyme to cells engaged in the synthesis of hyaluronic acid. A distortion of this synthesis results in the formation of an antigenic carbohydrate and to an irritant protein which gives rise to the clinical manifestation. Selye has done a great deal of work on the relation of endocrine disturbance to arthritis and likewise the effect of stress. The cause of rheumatoid arthritis is not explained by abnormal peripheral circulation, alteration in carbohydrate metabolism, specific foods or, for that matter, anything else. In 1948 it was confirmed that a specific substance of unknown nature, quite similar to an antibody, circulated in the blood of rheumatoid arthritics. A great deal of work has been carried on in the United States and Great Britain during the last decade to determine the exact nature of this substance which is call "the rheumatoid factor." Much has been done on the isolation of the "factor." The current thinking is that the rheumatoid factor causes the body to alter its state of immunity or autoimmunity and, probably with the addition of a genetic or metabolic predisposing factor, gives rise to definite symptoms of the disease.

Patients complain of malaise, fatigue, numbness and tingling in the extremities, loss of weight, exhaustion and general debility. Gradually one or

*Hyaluronic acid is a mucopolysaccharide found in synovial and subcutaneous tissue.

more joints, most often the interphalangeal joints of the fingers gradually become warm, painful or swollen. After that there is a symmetrical polyarticular distribution, and the joints show a spindle shaped appearance due to the thickening of the periarticular tissues and the atrophy of the surrounding muscles. The patient complains of pain, swelling and limitation of motion.

The joint involvement is often distributed symmetrically and there is a tendency for progression of the process from the peripheral joints toward the trunk. However, any joint in the body may become involved in the process. In the usual case, there is little systemic reaction except a very low grade fever and tachycardia with a mild loss of weight during the very early stages of the process. In the early stages it is difficult to distinguish the disease from rheumatic fever. There are almost fifty diseases which may be mistaken for rheumatoid arthritis. The early course of rheumatoid arthritis is characterized by remissions and relapses. As the disease progresses, joint pain and swelling increase and muscular stiffness becomes more marked. Muscular atrophy appears and there is a limitation of motion of the affected parts. However, the severity of the pain is no index of the ultimate progress. Pain, stiffness, limitation of motion and swelling are the main symptoms. Somehow or other, atmospheric changes cause an exacerbation of the disorder. Rheumatic patients have become to be known as weather vanes and prophets. No actual cause is known for this except that it is believed that such atmospheric changes as the fall in barometric pressure before a thunderstorm vary the electrical ion concentration of the air in a negative direction, causing an increased sensitivity of the sensory nerves. Unfavorable prognostic signs include a slow, insidious onset with involvement of fresh joints from time to time, a persistently high sedimentation rate, marked muscular atrophy, subcutaneous nodules, persistent loss of weight, persistent tachycardia; subcutaneous nodules may appear in from 5 to 25 per cent of patients with rheumatoid arthritis. Cold and clammy hands are common in patients with rheumatoid arthritis, but there, is, on occasion, a "hot house palm" with warm, moist hands.

The laboratory findings are fairly simple. There is a moderate or marked increase in the sedimentation rate, a moderate secondary anemia (due to decreased hemoglobin rather than red blood cell count), a moderate leukocytosis, primarily polys. There is usually positive agglutination of the patient's serum with strains of hemolytic strep in titer of 1:160 or more, but only after the case is well along for at least a year.

In some cases the onset and clinical picture resemble rheumatic fever so closely that the true nature of the disease is revealed only after the passage of considerable time.

The course of the disease usually runs over a period of years. The progress may be interrupted temporarily or permanently at any stage, so that no patient with rheumatoid arthritis should be considered as beyond aid.

Other tests useful in differential diagnoses are blood uric acid test, g.c. complement fixation test, B. abortus agglutination test, synovial fluid findings, joint culture and biopsy, basal metabolism rate, antistrepos lyn content of serum, antifibrinolysin, precipitins, Weltman coagulation, formal-gel reaction, blood culture and serum phosphatase. During the progression of rheumatoid arthritis, various changes may be seen by Roentgen examination. When slight swelling of the joint occurs, soft tissue films will disclose the increased periarticular width and density and also atrophy of the epiphyseal line. With increased atrophy, erosions and marginal bony exostoses may appear. Varying degrees of articular destruction are seen on the roentgenogram. In most cases there is marked decalcification, mostly in the hands and feet. In a large number of cases there is atrophic bone destruction (as exhibited by punched-out areas); likewise, effusion into the joint and narrowing and obliteration of the joint space and lipping and production of bone are seen in a goodly number of cases.

As yet there is no specific test which will differentiate rheumatic diseases from other similar disease.

TREATMENT

Most authorities agree that about half the victims of rheumatoid arthritis will eventually improve regardless of the form of treatment used. No simple method of treatment available currently has proven to have a long-lasting effect on the natural course of the disease. The first aim of treatment is the relief of symptoms, the second, the improvement of the patient's health, and finally, the restoration of function in the patient's affected joints.

In the acute stage, bed rest coupled with discrete exercise in the thoracic, lumbar and gluteal regions are advised. Analgesics and hypnotics prescribed in adequate doses, particularly aspirin, are used. Various local measures such as skin-tight plaster of Paris splints are also active measures to restore function and stability to the affected joints such as a stationary bicycle, rowing machine and graduated recreational activities play a useful part. Various forms of physiotherapy are used to supplement more active treatment. Occupational therapy can serve a purpose in restoring work endurance.

Chrysotherapy or gold salts has been reported in the literature as an effective therapeutic agent. It appears that the maximum therapeutic response to gold occurs during or following the first course of injections. Subsequent courses are less effective in controlling the activity of the disease. There have been reports of toxic reactions, but they were serious in only 5 per cent of the cases. The mode of action of gold salts is unknown, and benefit can only be obtained during the active phase of the disease. Usually the preparation of choice is a water-soluble gold salt given by intramuscular injection. Forester has reported good results from the intravenous use of copper salts in the treatment of rheumatoid arthritis. Other investigators have used bismuth and salazopyrin, a drug obtained by the chemical combination of salicylic acid and sulphapyridine, with varying results. Phenylbutazone, a powerful analgesic, leads to a subjective improvement in a high proportion of cases of rheumatoid arthritis. It has very little antirheumatic effect, the symptoms recurring soon after its withdrawal. It has certain side effects which should be watched for.

Hench and his colleagues at the Mayo Clinic reported the dramatic suppression of symptoms which followed the administration of Kendall's Compound E (cortisone) and adrenocorticotrophic hormone (ACTH) to patients suffering from rheumatoid arthritis. When cortisone or ACTH was stopped, signs of rheumatic activity usually returned rapidly, but in some cases symptoms remained absent for periods varying from two weeks to a few months. Undesirable side effects appeared in 60 per cent of the cases but were usually mild in the majority of cases and consisted of acne, slight hirsutism, rounding of the face and irritability. ACTH and cortisone do not have any curative effects. Both ACTH and cortisone are given intramuscularly, four to six hourly or intravenously slowly over twenty-four hours. Cortisone acetate is the preparation in general use both for oral and penetral treatment. Hydrocortisone (Compound F) has been used interchangeably with cortisone and ACTH with about the same results. Treatment with ACTH, cortisone and hydrocortisone is contraindicated in patients who are suffering from infection, tuberculosis, ulcers of the stomach or duodenum, hypertension, certain forms of renal and cardiac disease, psychotics, diabetics and osteoporosis.

Recently the United States Food and Drug Administration approved for medical prescription a drug developed by Doctor Normal Rothermich, Professor of Medicine at Ohio State University, and his associates, called indomethacin. It is related to tryptophane, one of the basic amino acids that somehow seems to go awry in rheumatoid arthritis. In their preliminary experimental studies, 75 per cent of the rheumatoid arthritis patients showed excellent or good improvement, and there were few side effects.

Improvement was measured by increased function, mobility of joints and relief of pain and swelling. The most common side effects were headache, lightheadedness and stomach upsets, which disappeared when the

Most recently a drug called Oraflex has been used with some success by arthritic patients, but it has as yet not been approved by the FDA, primarily because in some patients, it has produced insidious side effects.

PSYCHOLOGICAL AND PSYCHIATRIC ASPECTS OF RHEUMATOID ARTHRITIS

The psychological aspects of rheumatoid arthritis have had a long history, but it is only recently that this phase of the disease has been studied intensively. In 1937 and 1942 L. Halliday, the well-known English internist, published articles on this subject. Gordon in 1939 postulated the theory that there is an organ inferiority which localizes the disturbance of arthritis and that is the reason why the illness goes to one locus and not another. The recovery and freedom from relapse depends in a large measure on the patient's degree of emotional stability and on satisfactions on his philosophy of life. Halliday, in 1943, in discussing psychosomatic affections in general lists the various organ systems affected by emotional imbalance. One of the organ systems he speaks of is "locomotor system," and he says that many cases of fibrositis, neuritis, sciatica and lumbago, as well as postural defects such as scoliosis, lordosis and kyphosis are definitely of psychosomatic origin, while rheumatoid arthritis and nontraumatic osteoarthritis are of possible psychosomatic etiology. Halliday offered a five point formula for arthritis.

1. *Emotion*—In several investigations the proportion of upsetting external events is greater than in the controls.
2. *Personality*—Persons who develop rheumatoid arthritis show definite emotional limitations and self-restrictions. They tend to be independent and self-sufficient, keeping things to themselves. They are self-sacrificing and show obsessional trends and have obsessive-compulsive characteristics.
3. *Sex*—The incidence is three to five times more common in females than males.
4. *Associated Affections*—Psoriasis and iridocyclitis.
5. *Family History*—There is a positive family history in 30–40 per cent of the cases.

Johnson, Shapiro and Alexander give a series of psycho-dynamic findings in a study of thirty-three cases of rheumatoid arthritis, four males and twenty-nine females. The precipitating psychological factor of the disease has no common denominator. They cover a wide range of external and psychological significant events; in fact they run the whole gamut of life situations—the birth of a child, miscarriage, death in the family, change in occupation, sudden change in marital situation, etc. The men had a tendency toward bodily activity, manifesting itself in an inclination toward outdoor and competitive sports. The women in periods of latency and adolescence show a decidedly tom-boyish behavior. The females show a striking need to be of service to other people. In respect to their children all patients in this study are exacting and demanding. They do a great deal for their children but have a tendency to dominate them. The sexual behavior of all the female patients shows the common feature of an overt and easily recognizable rejection of the feminine role. They assume certain masculine attitudes, compete with men and cannot submit to them. There is an unconscious rebellion against men due to disappointments with them. These are precipitated by events which tend to increase hostility and guilt feelings, previously latent; these guilt feelings were adequately handled through the patient's self-sacrifice and service to others. The masculine protest reaction was intensified in order to serve as a defense against fear of sexual attack. The family situation presents a strong, domineering, demanding mother and more commonly a mild, gentle, compliant father. In the females, the female role becomes frightening with the oedipal period.

In general what happens is that the equilibrium of the patient is disturbed (between aggressive impulses and control); the chronic inhibited aggression leads to increased muscle tonus and in some way to arthritis. In a small number of cases, specific sexual conflicts are handled by typical symbolic conversion mechanism. In general the dynamic background is a chronic, inhibited, hostile aggressive state as a reaction to the earliest masochistic dependence on the mother that is carried on to father and all human relationships including the sexual. The majority of these personalities learn to discharge hostility through masculine competition, physical activity, serving and domination of the family. When the methods of discharge are interrupted in specific ways the persistent increased muscle tonus resulting from inhibited aggression and the defense against it in some way precipitates the arthritis.

The work of Ludwig, while at the National Institutes of Health, is interesting in regard to the psychiatric etiology of arthritis. He has studied arthritis rather extensively and claims that rheumatoid arthritics have a marked impairment of ego function manifested by extreme dependence, insecurity, feelings of inadequacy, difficulty in the usual methods of mastery or coping with the environment and with other people, severe block of external expression of emotion with internalization of feeling an autonomic overactivity. Arthritics, he claims, are unaware of their feelings of helplessness. They frequently deny their dependence by overcompensating with an outward facade of independence, self-assurance, self-control and apparent shallowness of emotion. With their security the world is a hostile place which constantly threatens to injure them. Strange people, new situations, even slight changes within a familiar environment may produce severe anxiety; anxiety is also produced by slightest criticism or real or apparent rejection. In a group studied by Ludwig the single most important precipitating factor was loss or separation from an important key figure on whom the patient depends for support. Ludwig believes that the first task of the therapist is to restore his sense of security. The therapist must take great pains not to react to the defensive hostility of the patient. Arthritics appear to be calm but in reality are bursting inside. There are two diametrically opposite ways that arthritics display their personality. First, there is the patient who remains in bed and won't get up. He is the parasite tyrannizing all medical and paramedical personnel. Then there is the patient who refuses all help; he attempts to deny his illness. Ludwig's studies of large numbers of patients at Massachusetts General Hospital showed increased sweating, cold hands, increased pulse rate and GI disturbances.

Cleveland and Fisher have made some interesting contributions to the psychological study of rheumatoid arthritis. In a project involving both rheumatoid arthritics and ulcer patients they found that in arthritics there is a conflict centered about the curtailment of strong hostile feelings. Prior to the onset of arthritis there was a diversion of these impulses into vigorous muscular exercise such as competitive sports and rough outdoor activity. They also have a unique body image emphasizing the containing and protective aspects of the body boundary. Pride in their physique and strong unconscious exhibitionistic desires contribute to the picture. The females prior to their illness had an interest in cooking and other household duties. On the Holtzman Ink Blot Test there was a tendency for the arthritics to emphasize the containing and protective character of their body image exterior. These special body image fantasies are not mere reflections of symptom discomfort but represent basic styles of orientation toward one's body and toward one's environment.

Fisher and Cleveland, in assessing the personality of arthritics before, during and after ACTH therapy, found these arthritics to have a better than average IQ; previous ACTH projective tests indicated the patients to be hostile, dependent individuals whose ability to express aggression was quite limited. They were immature sexually and afraid to express their sexual impulses. They exhibited compulsive and hysterical neurotic defense mechanisms.

There was constant monitoring of inner life manifested by a high degree of egocentricity and lack of genuine interest and warmth toward persons other than themselves. The men were strikingly alike in their personality patterns, withdrew from difficult situations, were passively effeminate, sought dependent relationships with father figures and were covertly hostile toward a disapproving mother.

The pre-ACTH psychiatric diagnoses were schizoid personality, compulsive personality, hysterical character and conversion hysteria.

Nearly all the patients in this group, while receiving ACTH, reacted as though they had developed more aggressive push or energy. The response to this increase in aggressive energy seemed to be intensified use of the old defenses which were characteristic of the patient. Those who improved the most tended to express their aggressiveness more freely and with less guilt in effective problem solving behavior. With moderate amounts of ACTH patients who were inclined to discharge anger verbally in sarcasm or barbed humor do so more and with added effectiveness. Others who used blandness and denial of affect became more controlled and uncommunicative.

In three patients in whom 60–80 mgm of ACTH failed to produce significant joint improvement, the dosage was increased to 90–230 mgm daily. In all three instances there occurred no physiological improvement, but there occurred a breakdown of the old defense patterns with agitation, anxiety, and agitated depression severe enough in two instances to require psychiatric hospitalization.

Six of the ten patients who habitually remembered their dreams continued to dream while on ACTH, and coincidentally these experienced the best clinical response to ACTH. The dream material concerned with conflicts apparently became more acceptable and could be dealt with more readily.

Most of the patients who gave more direct expression to their hostility during the ACTH treatment were among the improved cases. Contrarily, those expressing less direct hostility during therapy tended to remain unimproved. Some patients in the improved group showed less self-accusation during therapy and in none was this attitude exaggerated while the patient was on ACTH. The unimproved patients demonstrated greater self-accusation while receiving ACTH.

On the Rosenzweig Picture Frustration Test, most of the patients who gave more direct expression to hostility during ACTH treatment were among the improved cases. Contrarily, those expressing less direct hostility during therapy tended to remain unimproved. In seven unimproved patients, the pathological personality tendencies noted in the first test became exaggerated during ACTH treatment. This distortion did not occur in any patients who showed clinical improvement. Both the improved and the unimproved patients demonstrated an intensification of neurotic elements. Greater withdrawal tendencies were seen in three of the improved patients but in none of the unimproved patients. Compulsive patterns increased in both groups. Freer use of emotional expression occurred in seven of the improved patients and in only two of the unimproved.

In general the patients who improved under ACTH treatment became better able to express their feelings directly. At the same time these patients were able to make better use of their neurotic mechanisms that permitted them to be less sensitive to impinging situations. Clinically, the unimproved patient became more tense, felt that he must react to environmental pressure, but was unable to discharge emotions any better than before. The resulting pressure may account for the fact that the gross personality distortions were seen only in patients who did not improve. ACTH seems to enhance or restore the aggressiveness of the patient, perhaps because the psychic component of adaptation in arthritics involved the tendency to take action against the stress agent. The patient's response seems to be in terms of his habitual attitude regarding his own aggression. The control of aggression may be handled with repressive techniques. ACTH seems to restore the patient's physiological and psychological capacity to bear the stress in a way that is pharmacological and includes, but goes beyond, pain relief and the simple satisfaction of a dependent needs implicit in this or any form of supportive therapy. This restoration alone may be enough to raise the patient from his state of relative exhaustion if the stresses are not too great at the time of treatment. Or this reparative effect may fail if the stresses are so severe that the difference between the stress and the impaired capacity to meet it are too great to be eliminated by the ACTH effect. The action of ACTH seems to include the supportive, stress relieving potentialities of other forms of therapy but seems to go further in its direct addition to the psychophysiological capacity of the patient to adapt.

The data from this study indicates that the emotional as well as physical responses of arthritics to ACTH were related to the nature and quantity of stresses under which the patient was operating at the time of treatment. The most satisfactory clinical physiological response seemed to occur in those individuals whose precipitating stresses had been quite severe, so that the stresses at the time of treatment were relatively mild.

In another study Cleveland and Fisher found that in interviewing arthritics, they appeared overtly to be calm, composed and optimistic individuals who rarely if ever express or even feel hostility. When hostility is expressed it goes inward. They complain of their own social shyness and social inadequacy. They report that preceding the arthritic involvement they had an intense interest and participation in sports. They also had an intense involvement with cooking and household duties. The mother was seen as an excellent housekeeper, compulsively clean and efficient; the mother was also seen as a disciplinarian. The father was inconsistent in behavior. He was strong and weak at the same time. Their self-image was one of having a body which was a hollow chamber. The chamber was found to be surrounded by hard, dense material. Cleveland and Fisher believe that this body image mirrors a mode of defense which arthritics adapt to protect themselves against unacceptable, hostile impulses. Rheumatoid arthritics are fearful of their own anger, resentments and hostilities. The authors believe that hunting and fishing can serve as satisfactory sublimations for their anger. In giving these arthritics the Rorschach, the authors found that arthritics think of their body as a kind of hollow container filled with uncontrolled fluid material and surrounded by hard, impenetrable surface. Inconsistent parents seem to have supplied the original model for the body image.

Southworth has postulated the theory that the muscle tension in arthritics is caused by one of two things:

1. The arthritic patient tends to maintain after a stressful experience the psychological disturbance that was produced during stress. This could serve to keep the arthritic psychosomatic union (of which psychological stress and heightened muscle tension are a part) activated; or
2. In arthritic patients, once the heightened muscle tension is initiated psychologically, it can persevere for awhile in an autonomous manner with respect to the original psychological stimulus. If the muscle tension persists for a prolonged period of time or occurs frequently, then this tension could serve as a mechanical stress on the joints connected with the muscles. What may take place in a joint that is stressed by prolonged muscle tension is an inflammatory condition that is directly caused by a nonadaptive hormonal response to the physiological stress of heightened muscle tension, and this chain of events may have been initiated by psychological stress. The author postulates the theory that the arthritic process could begin with conscious aggressive impulses that become intolerable. If the "hard shell" of muscle tension was once consciously erected against the disturbing aggression, and then the whole conflict was repressed, we have inhibited aggression as a prominent feature in an essentially hysterically initiated illness. In a

comparison of arthritic patients with ulcer patients, arthritics tend to be more disturbed in their relationships with their parents than ulcer patients. Arthritics tend to show more strain in their relationship with their mother than ulcer patients.

In a searching article on rheumatoid arthritics, Stanley King delineated what he thought were the common factors of the personalities of rheumatoid arthritics. They:

1. Lead quiet lives;
2. Complain of shyness and inadequacy;
3. Have marked feelings of inadequacy and inferiority;
4. Are self-sacrificing;
5. Are overconscientious;
6. Have a strong need to serve others;
7. Have obsessive-compulsive characteristics;
8. Have a tendency to depression.

The most prominent problem is that of aggression. Both children and adults are described as having a strong reservoir of hostility below consciousness, primitive in nature with sadistic and destructive fantasies. However, the arthritic is fearful of his anger and resentments, fearful that expression of these feelings will have drastic consequences for him. This may account for his emotional self-restriction and his inability to show anger. Confirming the work of other investigators, King has shown that arthritics are keenly perceptive of other people's feelings, allowing themselves to be imposed upon rather than risking offending and so losing the regard of others. It is suggested by King that arthritics have a fear of separation, especially from key figures on whom he depends, and this difficulty began in childhood with an extreme mother-child interdependence. The final personality conflict seems to be in the area of sexual identification and adjustment with a high incidence of voyeuristic fantasies.

King divides the mechanisms by which emotion or interpretations of environmental events are related to the physiological changes of the disease into three types.

1. *Muscle Tension*—Rheumatoid arthritics reflect psychological tensions and conflicts through variations in tensions and in the somatic muscular system.
2. *Symbolic Manifestations*—The symptoms of rheumatoid arthritis may be in some manner symbolic manifestation of conflict, e.g., localization of the disease seems to be in the joints in which the conflict was focused, e.g., soldiers get a swelling of the lower extremities.

3. *Symbolic Control*—Arthritis symptoms represent a means of controlling or preventing the expression of hostile, aggressive impulses—that if the joints are stiff and rigid, motion is limited, anger will be encapsulated and danger to others and to the patient will be averted.

In doing Rorschach studies of male arthritics, King showed that many of the pathological features usually seen in the psychotic personality, including continuation and confabulatory responses, color naming and extensive poor form level, are characteristic of arthritics.

Boland uses the term "psychogenic rheumatism" which is the musculoskeletal expression of functional disorders, tension states of psychoneurosis. Psychic disturbances alone cannot cause the disorder. Grief and anxiety may occasionally precipitate the experience and in some cases appears to be temporarily related to fluctuations in the clinical course of rheumatoid arthritis. Thus emotional upsets may be the "trigger mechanisms" of the disease, but the body harbors the causative factor. The diagnosis of "psychogenic rheumatism" is not made by excluding organic disease but by:

1. Absence of organic disease or insufficient disease to account for the disability;
2. Qualitative functional characteristics of the disability; and
3. Positive diagnosis of psychopathology.

According to Boland, psychogenic rheumatism may be divided into three types:

1. *Pure*—When clinical, lab, and roentgenogram evidence of organic joint disease or muscle abnormality is lacking;
2. *Superimposed*—When incapacitating psychogenic symptoms are associated with nondisabling organic changes; and
3. *Residual*—When the disability is perpetuated due to functional symptoms which take over after the disease process has subsided.

The relative frequency of these subdivisions based on 1021 cases of psychogenic rheumatism in the Army and Navy is enumerated below.

Pure	41.6%
Superimposed	39.5%
Residual	18.9%

The most common symptoms of psychogenic rheumatism are "pain," "tenseness," subjective sense of swelling, muscle fatigue and weakness of an involved part. These complaints are more often generalized all over but may predominate in one region or another. They sometimes are vague in quality or location. The pain has a "functional" characteristic, i.e., it may be fleeting or constant, bad all the time, present day or night, etc. The distribution of the pain is not anatomical, i.e., it is not restricted to any one area. The patient may not have pain at all, but merely parasthesia. There are associated functional characteristics such as headache, dyspnea, globus, sighing, apnea, anxiety, nervousness, etc. present. In practically all cases there is evidence of previous neurotic traits, e.g., enuresis, somnambulism, nightmares, temper tantrums, morbid fears, stammering fainting spells, etc. are frequent. The localization of the symptom is prompted by the past or present experience or by expediency. He probably had a history of traumatic or inflammatory joint disease in his past. By this reasoning, Halliday argues that if examples of stomach trouble existed, it is probable that functional dyspepsia rather than psychogenic rheumatism would have developed in response to the same emotional stress.

In another article Halliday attempts to differentiate between a true fibrositis and what he calls "psychoneurotic rheumatism." Fibrosis is a disease characterized by subjective complaints of localized pain and stiffness. They are commonly related to localized objective findings such as nodules, thickenings and indurations which result from inflammation of fibrous tissue and fossa. The etiology is obscure, but the nodules can be palpated and also can be located by gross and microscopic pathological examination. Psychogenic rheumatism on the other hand comes from "upset in emotions" which bring about subjective symptoms of pain, stiffness and limitation of movement which appear on medical certificates under such names as muscular rheumatism, fibrositis, sciatica, neuritis, lumbago and pleurodynia. Halliday believes that there is a close relationship between hysteria and threats to bodily preservation.

Cleveland and Fisher take this one step further and try to relate the malfunctioning of specific organs with psychodynamics. They postulate the theory that life experiences which an individual has with his body gradually builds up a body schema which influences how the body will be used to express conflicts and disturbances. According to their schema arthritics unconsciously conceive of their body as a container whose walls are formed out of a hard protective substance. They fantasy their outer body wall as a tough defensive barrier designed to ward off threats from the outside and to hold disturbing hostile impulses from the interior. Thus people whose psychosomatic symptoms involve the body exterior would conceive of their bodies as surrounded by a protective, defensive wall, whereas those with symptoms involving the body interior would conceive of their bodies as lacking a defensive wall and being easily penetrated. They did experimental work with Rorschachs in this area.

Weiss in working with five women and thirty-five men with various muscular complaints (arthritis, fibrositis, muscular and nonarticular rheumatism, tuberculosis and rheumatic fever) found the following psychiatric distribution of these patients.

Hysteria	16
Anxiety State	11
Hypochondriasis	2
Psychotic Depression	2
Neurotic Character Disorder	9

He found that poor sleep, poor sexual adjustment and marital problems were prevalent.

A special feature associated with muscular aches was chronic resentment. These patients are "burned up" with resentment and "aching" to express their unappeased hostility. Smouldering resentment is a special feature of patients with muscular aches and pains. When these patients were asked what they thought was the cause of their illness, they invariably answered marital incompatibility and sexual difficulties.

It is interesting to note that there is very little relationship between arthritis and psychoses. In an unselected group of 360 chronic mental hospital patients over the age of forty, only 18 per cent had rheumatoid arthritis. The authors explain this on a hereditary basis. Both diseases may result from an inherent defect which may be mutually exclusive.

Teiger's studies on psychogenic rheumatism show that the diffuse, shifting pain which is experienced is something peculiar and personal to the patient. Such patients, he says, are exhibitionistic and physically very tense and find it almost impossible to relax. On physical examination they may react in one or two diametrically opposite ways. They may either resist or resent examination or they may exhibit the "self-prodding phenomenon" and even seize the doctor's fingers and plunge them into the so-called tender areas. In fact, these tender areas are often mistaken for fibrositis and are areas of cutaneous hyperesthesia with no organic involvement whatsoever. Teiger believes that in these instances the rheumatism is an attention-getting device. These patients do not respond well to oral analgesics. Local injection of anesthetics, while it may produce temporary alleviation of localized symptoms, are almost invariably accompanied by extraordinary general manifestations such as fainting, palpitation and disorientation.

Why does the rheumatoid arthritic "choose" the musculoskeletal system for expression of somatic symptoms? Halliday believes that the fixation is prompted by the past or present environmental experiences or by expediency. Gordon, on the other hand, believes that there is an organ inferiority which localizes the disturbance and its effects and that is the reason why illness goes to one locus and not another. In addition to organ inferiority Halliday believes that the illness may strike as a result of symbolism, e.g., a feeling of resistance in the posterior midline either at the back of the neck between scapula or in lumbar regions, and such pains often symbolize inward feelings of resistance, obstinacy, and resentment. Pains in the arms and legs associated with numbness, tingling, deadness, and loss of power may symbolize repressed desire to attack.

PSYCHOSOCIAL FACTORS

At the Institute of Rehabilitation Medicine, at New York University, thirty-seven rheumatoid arthritic patients (twenty-five white and four Negro, two thirds Catholic) were selected for social analysis. They were interviewed by a social worker and psychologist initially. A comprehensive history was obtained of their psychosocial development from early childhood to the onset of arthritis and subsequent adjustments to their illness. The psychologist gave:

1. Wechsler-Bellevue;
2. TAT, Rorschach and Figure Drawings; and
3. Kuder and Purdue Pegboard.

The mean age of this group was thirty-six years. Ten of the patients were still married. Almost 50 per cent of the patients had restricted heterosexual relations. One third of the patients never got married and for one third the marriage was not permanent.

The most outstanding feature was the high incidence of changes in the family structure. For only nine of twenty-nine patients did the family structure remain stable throughout early childhood. In twenty-two patients the maternal attitude was negative, and in twenty-one the paternal attitude was negative. Most frequently the mothers had been dominating and controlling and the father passive, ineffective and uninterested and rarely available.

Most of these patients attributed their illness to a variety of causes but most often related it to other health problems or to environmental factors such as poor working conditions, over-exertion, accidents, tight shoes, etc. Most of the patients did not spontaneously refer to emotional traumata in their lives, but in discussing their life histories, the chronological relationship of such traumata to the onset of symptoms was noted. In five of the patients the arthritis followed childbirth or began concurrently with responsibilities to child care, and in three others it started at the time these patients became engaged or just after marriage. Several patients described conflicts with authority, particularly employers, just before the onset of the arthritis.

PSYCHOSOCIAL CONSEQUENCE OF ILLNESS

In every patient the development of arthritis caused changes in nearly every area of their lives from employment to recreational activities. In nearly every instance the illness functioned as a defense for the patient against his environment by promoting a punishment of self or family, a means of enforcing environmental control or a means of establishing or justifying dependence. For several patients the arthritis provided a satisfactory excuse for his withdrawal from his environment and an adequate rationalization for feelings of inadequacy.

These investigators analyzed six "failures" and six "successes" in rehabilitation. The following is a classification of the kinds of elements in those who were successful. The failures were opposite in the types of elements.

1. They are second-generation American of poor socio-economic status and moderate religious practice.
2. They are capable of handling heterosexual conflicts and taking decisive action in terminating their marital relationships where there was discord.
3. They began employment early without direct pressure and maintained a very good work history.
4. Economically, they attained a fair or reasonable standard of living.
5. They were financially independent five years before their illness.
6. Their disability was not as severe as the unsuccessful rehabilitates.
7. Their goal in rehabilitation was specific and realistic.

Very little work has been done hitherto on children affected with arthritis. Blom and Nichols believe that the onset, recurrence and speed of recovery of arthritis in children is greatly influenced by emotional factors. They studied twenty-eight children, ages two to sixteen, twenty-three girls and five boys, and observed that the onset seemed to occur during the initial phases in the emotional development of the child. Two thirds of the cases occurred in connection with an emotionally charged event. In one fourth of the cases they were able to demonstrate a recurrence of aggravation of arthritis in relation to an emotionally charged situation which was usually similar to the circumstances at the time of the original onset.

In regard to these children, the mothers were almost always guilty about the onset of the arthritis. The predominant theme seemed to be that because of the mother's illness or unhappiness during pregnancy, the child was affected and rheumatoid arthritis resulted.

In most instances hospitalization brought a severe reaction—separation from home resulted in a marked depressive attitude and feelings of abandonment and desertion. The children reacted to medical procedures in a fearful way or thought of them as punishment. The mother's separation from the child was an acutely upsetting experience for both, and the area in which the mothers showed the greatest concern was in the *eating of the child.* In those cases where there was an unusual dependency of the child on the mother, it was ascertained that this dependency antedated the illness but was fostered by the illness.

The personality characteristics of both mothers and children were ascertained as a group. In general:

1. The mothers were deeply deprived from childhood;
2. Over half the mothers experienced fear or were threatened by an important relative during the pregnancy or in the early life of the arthritic child; and
3. There was a marked tendency to depression, varying from acute depression to a mood of resignation and fatalistic stoical acceptance of whatever fate provides.

In general:

1. All the children showed a marked disturbance in mood and were unable to express their feelings;
2. Their fantasy life was of the primitive, aggressive, sadistic type;
3. Many had feeding difficulties;
4. Six children expressed poison fantasies; and
5. There was extreme ambivalence extending to many areas of conflict.

These authors believe that we are dealing with an infantile personality structure growing out of a long sustained conflict situation where the outstanding element is the inability of the child to achieve separation from the mother.

A good summary of the findings on arthritics was done by Bennett in a master's thesis at McGill University. The author's avowed purpose was to discover the influences, stresses, tensions and adjustments in the social field of the patient and how these are related to the precipitation, course, outcome and possible prevention of the illness. Bennett studied eighty rheumatoid arthritis patients from three clinics of three mental hospitals in Montreal, Canada. The study was conducted by four social workers under the direction of two psychiatrists and a professor at the McGill School of Social Work. Bennett summarizes the following from the literature on arthritics.

1. People developing rheumatoid arthritis have difficulty forming satisfying relationships with other people. They are unable to commit themselves in any love relationship and remain relatively detached even from those whom they are intimately related to. They have difficulty in controlling their temper and try to avoid situations which would require them to exercise foresight and restraint before asserting themselves.
2. Inability of these people to accept any situation which deprives them of independence is very marked, and the struggle to maintain independence is continued through the course of their illness.
3. When faced with a problem they cannot think it through—they tend first to resort to action which consists of generalized non-goal-directed muscular activity such as general restlessness.
4. They rely to a great extent on muscular activity to provide pleasurable tension release as borne out by pursuits in which they have engaged, e.g., swimming, skating, etc.

Of the arthritics which Bennett used, he studied, in addition to other elements, their employment. The single patients had a lower incidents of employment, and more than half the married females were at some time gainfully employed in addition to their occupation as housewife. The arthritics were employed in kinds of jobs which require the least possible contact and cooperation in which responsibility and concomitant anxiety are avoided and in which things, rather than people, and physical, rather than mental, efforts are involved. Most of these patients changed jobs to those kinds of occupations where they are their own bosses. Most of these people had a strong feeling of responsibility and tend to remain on the job during their illness, are meticulous and critical about getting their work done. They are also very sensitive about criticism, tend to escape trouble by hard work, very critical of their colleagues at work and are defiant of authority but repress this defiance. There was not much information obtained about relationship of these patients with their families, primarily because they did not assess this area very much. Most said their parents were strict and good and some said they were quick tempered. The loss of a parent by death or separation was a cause of added anxiety to half the patients while they were still adolescents. In general the marital relationships of these patients were generally inadequate and unsatisfactory because of unsatisfactory sexual adjustments. The strict moralistic attitude towards sex expression and the consequent ignorance, fear and psychological incapacity appear to underlie the dominating independence of the female patients and was chosen by some male patients. The female patients were subject to abuse and self-condemnation because pendence of the female patients and was chosen by some male patients. The female patients were subject to abuse and self-condemnation because of this frustration. Marriage to many of these patients was a form of escape, and runaway marriages and marriages without the knowledge or consent of the parents were quite common. Three fourths of these patients reported some stressful event or condition chronologically related to their illness. These stresses ranged from death of a loved one to intense anxiety over marital discord, sexual problems, etc.

In my work with rheumatoid arthritis patients and comparing them with a group who had an "internal syndrome" as opposed to the "external syndrome" with a questionnaire and a series of psychological tests, the MMPI, the Holtzman, and a group Rorschach, I found that the universal psychological elements of these patients were unexpressed rage and lack of ego strength. There also seemed to be no evidence of symbolic localization of specific joints. The results of the study shows that much of the etiology is congenital, both in the physical and psychological areas. This predisposition based on heredity undergoes modifications due to experiences beginning with the prenatal period and extending to adulthood and modified by stress during the life cycle. The congenital somatic factor not only determines psychological development but the psychological development defines the circumstances which may activate the pathology. In the case of the rheumatoid arthritics a rheumatoid factor isolated by Engelman at the University of California Medical Center in San Francisco, possibly determines the predisposition to the disease. Thus, if it is assumed that both ego strength and the rheumatoid factor are congenital and in a given person there is the presence of the rheumatoid factor and a weak ego plus the personality dynamics expressed heretofore, there is the likelihood of the rheumatoid arthritis developing.

DERMATOSES

DERMATOLOGICAL AILMENTS

It is generally considered that there are some dermatological ailments that may be considered psychosomatic. I chose to study four of these* acne vulgaris, atopic dermatitis, eczema of the hands, and psoriasis. These diseases (100 subjects each) were studied with their psychosomatic implications, with the MMPI, the Rorschach, and the Draw A Person

*See Geist, H.—Emotional Aspects of Dermatitis Journal of Clinical and Experimental Psychopathology, 18, 1, Jan–March 1957, 87–94.

image, had sexual difficulties, and a tendency to conversion symptoms and had a schizophrenic diathesis. The patients with atopic dermatitis were aggressively hostile, anxious and had disturbances in the sexual area. They had paranoid fantasies with a disturbance called psychological impotency or an inability to face their environmental realistically. The patients with eczema of the hands were very self conscious of their hands, had difficulty with authority, had a tendency to develop hysterical conversion symptoms and had difficulty in the sexual area. The patients with psoriasis had the most serious psychopathology, including depression, egocentricity, sensitivity, obsessive compulsive traits and sexual disturbances—they were also found to have prolific fantasy production and schizophrenic trends.

The following chart is a summary of the psychological test results of these patients.

DATA OBTAINED FOR EACH DIAGNOSTIC GROUP

MMPI	Rorschach	Draw A Person	Summary
Acne Vulgaris			
1. Seven scales with a mean *T* score of more than 60. Range is from a 49 *MF* scale to a *T* score of 67 in Schizophrenia and Hypomania. 2. In the psychotic triad, Psychastenia and Schizophrenia scales were high; in the neurotic triad, Depression and Hysteria scales were high but were lower than the two highest scales of the psychotic triad. 3. Psychopathic tendencies. 4. Conversion symptoms developed because of dermatologic ailment.	1. Lack of color responses. 2. Introtensive psychographic. 3. Schizophrenic responses in several records.	1. Majority of patients drew head only. 2. Profile drawing common. 3. Signs of sexual disturbance.	1. Psychoneurotic with over-productive thought content. 2. Relate poorly to own body image. 3. Sexual difficulties. 4. Schizophrenic diathesis. 5. Tendency to develop conversion symptoms.
Atopic Dermatitis			
1. Highest peaks in Psychasthenia and Hysteria scales. 2. Neurotic pattern with obsessive compulsive element	1. Aggressive pattern (*FM:M* = 3:1). 2. Free floating and intellectualized anxiety. 3. In 50% of cases, Card VI rejected. 4. Fantasy and "distanciation" responses.	1. Hostile and paranoid. 2. Insecurity.	1. Aggressively hostile and anxious, with distrubance in sexual area. 2. Fantasy and paranoid tendencies accompanying psychological impotency.
Eczema of Hand			
1. Within normal limits except for moderately elevated Hysteria scale. 2. Tendency to develop conversion symptoms.	1. Relatively "normal" except for rigid personality makeup.	1. All figures had hands in pockets.	1. Difficulty in sexual area. 2. Difficulty with authority. 3. Self-conscious of hands. 4. Tendency to develop hysteria conversion symptoms.
Psoriasis			
1. High Lie score. 2. High Hypochondriasis score.	1. Anxiety and conflict indicators. 2. Sensitivity, egocentricity, and depression. 3. Card VI rejected by two-thirds of patients and Card VII by three-fourths of this group.	1. Rigidly symmetrical figures.	1. Marked psychopathology including depression, egocentricity, sensitivity, sexual disturbance, intellectualized anxiety, and obsessive compulsive characterization. 2. Prolific fantasy production and schizophrenic trends.
Cellulitis			
1. High Lie and *Pd* score.	1. Constricted and rigid pattern. 2. Aggression and anxiety.	1. Tendency to omit or hide the hands.	1. Relative absence of psychopathology except for mild aggression and anxiety and a tendency to fabricate to achieve own ends. 2. Tendency to focus on parts of body afflicted.

CHAPTER 2

HEART DISEASE

EMOTIONAL ASPECTS OF HEART DISEASE

Disease of the heart is one of America's greatest national problems. It is estimated that 10–12 million Americans suffer from the more serious diseases of the heart and circulation, while 15 million are afflicted with less serious diseases. The economic toll of cardiovascular disability is overwhelming. Almost 700,000 man-years are lost in industry each year because of cardiovascular disabilities. This loss of man-years is equivalent to almost three billion dollars in earnings by those disabled by heart disease, and 450 million in federal income tax revenue. With this money the federal government could have provided 60,000 fully equipped high schools. Industrial absenteeism in the United States resulting from cardiovascular disease and its complications is surpassed in incidence only by respiratory disease. In a worldwide survey it was found that one out of every six cardiac patients fails to return to work for psychological reasons, even after being told by his physician that he is in good health. If this is so, then about 200,000 people are so affected since about a million and a half people in this country suffer myocardial infarction each year—with about one million deaths.

CLASSIFICATION OF HEART DISEASE

Heart disease has so many manifestations; it is one of the few illnesses which presents unusual obstacles to orderly classification. However, the New York Heart Association developed a relatively simple classification of the functional status of cardiac patients which is now accepted and used by a wide variety of clinicians. Patients are divided into four classes:

- Class I — Patients who have organic heart disease, but can perform all customary activities without significant symptoms.
- Class II — Patients who have symptoms when performing ordinary, moderately strenuous activities; they tolerate less than ordinary activities well and are comfortable at rest.
- Class III — Patients who are restricted by symptoms so that less than ordinary activities, even minor ones, produce discomfort; they are comfortable at rest.

Class IV Patients who can perform no physical activities without some discomfort and usually have symptoms at rest as well.

This is a very subjective classification made primarily from what the patient tells the physician. It may or may not be reliable.

Selzer, on the other hand, has devised what he calls a "therapeutic" classification of heart disease and has divided this into the following:

A. Patients are permitted to undertake unlimited physical effort.
B. Patients' only restriction concerns avoidance of severe or competitive effort.
C. Patients' ordinary physical activities are moderately restricted and strenuous activities eliminated altogether.
D. Patients are permitted to engage only in minor activities.
E. Patients are placed on a rest regimen, confined to bed or chair.

These represent a functional classification insofar as activity is concerned. However, the best classification seems to be in the areas of etiology and structural abnormalities supplemented by physiological disorders. These are determined by cardiac catheterization techniques.*

There is a dearth of literature and even less experimental evidence on the emotional aspects of heart disease. There is more information on effect than cause. Despite the folklore—that the heart is the traditional seat of the emotions and much in literature linking the heart with courage, love, hate, etc., ("love comes from the heart," People are "soft-hearted," show "heartfelt sympathy" or are "heartless," the heart may be "bursting with joy" or "weighs on the heart," or one may die of a "broken heart,") experimental evidence of any link is hard to come by. Freud (34) called attention to the heart in connection with anxiety attacks and also in connection with various mild disorders of the heart, such as tachycardia, palpitation, and various arrhythmias, but this was purely speculation. Weiss uses the term "cardiac neurosis" where anxiety causes various abnormalities of the heart such as hypertension, various valvular defects, and what he calls "neurocirculatory asthenia." Wendkos has shown alterations in the T-wave in the precordial lead in patients with neurocirculatory asthenia which cannot be distinguished from those with angina heart disease. Weiss has claimed that the pain of hypertensives and those with headaches are of the same origin. Repressed hostility (Weiss also calls it chronic rage and inhibited aggression) seems to bear a definite relationship to hypertension, and when this hostility is turned "outward," anxiety is diminished and blood pressure

---

*The classification here is one recommended by Selzer, Arthur; The Heart—Its Function in Health and Disease, University of California Press, 1966.

is often lowered. Wolf and Wolff in studying patients with and without structural diseases of the heart note the following:

> "Heart pain in the presence of anatomical narrowing of the coronary arteries may result from increased work of the heart attendant upon prolonged elevation of the blood pressure and cardiac output in association with rage, resentment, anxiety, fear and tension."

They go on to say "heart pain in the presence of anatomical narrowing of the arteries may result from a fall in cardiac output and coronary blood flow in association with desperation and defeat." The latter is known as the "hypodynamic" response.

PSYCHOTHERAPY

The literature on psychotherapy with cardiacs is practically nonexistent primarily because it has been attempted so rarely. Stine describes short-term psychotherapy with patients who suffered coronary insufficiency, coronary occlusion, and cardiac arrest resulting in acute anxiety and depression. Brief psychotherapy consisted of keeping the treatment goals limited to symptom relief or restoration to a previous level of functioning, early institution of treatment as soon after symptoms as possible, and focus on precipitating stress. Important elements in treatment are the early formulation of the clinical material and focusing on denial as the primary defense, attention to the narcissistic injury created by the illness or trauma, and emphasis on the cognitive understanding of the patient and of his illness.

Hickan, Cargill, and Golden studied cardiovascular reaction to emotional stimuli and showed that in the majority of persons anxiety has an effect on the circulatory system similar to that produced by small doses of epinephrine.

The personality of patients with coronary artery disease has been pretty extensively studied. It might be pertinent to review these research projects.

Dunbar in her monumental work in psychosomatic medicine, has delineated some of the characteristics of *her* coronary patients. There was a high illness record, a high marriage rate, they came from large families, they stuck to one job, they worked long hours without vacation under stress and strain, there was little interest in sports, there were no hobbies, and a marked interest in intellectual activities. As children they had a tendency to be stubborn and self-willed and a tendency to brood. Their early competitive relationships were with a much feared and envied parent. Their chief defense mechanisms were repression and identification.

They drove themselves compulsively through hard work and self discipline but success brought no gratification or relief from tension.

Arlow has made several studies on coronary patients. He describes the coronary patient as a stubborn self-willed child who very early entered into a competitive relationship with a much feared and envied parent. The conflict is repressed as an identification is made with this parent. In his work relations, there is an overwhelming drive toward success. There is also a tremendous drive toward equalling superiors and dominating others. Success does not bring with it a sense of gratification or relief from tension. The coronary individual is constantly drawn into new situations where he recreates again and again the original situation of competition. The inner insecurity and sense of weakness which these kinds of patients experience and which they deny, remains unaffected by realistic achievements. The coronary individual constantly needs new successes to alleviate his own doubts.

Miles, Waedfogel, Barrabbee and Cobb studied 46 coronary patients and 49 controls in Boston. Each coronary patient and control was given a psychiatric interview of 1-1/2 hours, a Rorschach, the 16 P F questionnaire, the Otis Mental Ability Test and their social history was reviewed. There was little discernable difference in the intensity of neurotic disturbances in the two groups, although the coronary patients tended to utilize repression to a greater degree than the controls. There was a close correlation between the character structure of the patient and his subsequent life adaptation. It was interesting that there were many more cases of cardiovascular disease reported in the families of coronary patients than in the controls; there was a two times greater incidence of histories suggesting coronary artery disease among relatives of coronary patients than in the controls, suggesting a strong familial diathesis in coronary artery disease. The coronary patients also seem less reflective than the controls. They are much more interested in action than reflection and have little awareness of their inner feelings. Coronary patients also have difficulty in handling their aggressive feelings.

Gildea has summarized the views of many writers on the behavior patterns and personality factors in patients with coronary artery disease.

1. Great need for respect for authority
2. An unremitting worker
3. They stick to one occupation
4. They are invariably business executives or officials
5. They are compulsive
6. Have relatively little awareness of bodily symptoms
7. Have feelings of insecurity and inferiority

8. The work or job is a defense against anxiety
9. They are sociable and well liked.

Dr. Paul D. White, the late noted cardiologist, has made a rather plebeian but interesting note on the spiritual and physical attributes of the heart patients. He says that various kinds of heart abnormalities such as cardiac enlargement, permanent arrhythmia, tachycardia, paroxymal or permanent auricular fibrillation or flutter, prolonged auricular tachycardia or heart failure may be due to emotional reasons. The most common influence of mind on the body is simple fear of heart disease. Neurocirculatory asthenia is frequently superimposed on structural heart disease. The various disorders of rhythm which may sometimes be set off by emotion may in turn cause great mental stress and on occasion have been responsible for serious neuroses.

There have been some attempts to compare the personalities of patients with various kinds of heart disease. Kemple compared the personality traits of patients with rheumatic disease, hypertensive cardiovascular disease, coronary occlusion and fracture.

The rheumatics (presumably rheumatoid arthritics) show "dominant passivity and lack of aggressive drive." Many of these patients are active, energetic and even compulsively industrious. They do not identify with strong or dominant figures but with a weak dependent figure. Many of the males showed a feminine identification, a confusion about sexual roles with feelings of sexual inadequacy. In both sexes there is a prevalence of instinctive weakness and repression. Many of these patients feel acutely hostile and resentful toward various pressures in their environment and none of them find any satisfactory outlet for this hostility. Geist in his extensive study of rheumatoid arthritics found that inhibited aggression is the most outstanding trait of rheumatoid arthritics.

The patients with hypertensive vascular disease, on the other hand, showed a much greater need to achieve, dominate, and be respected. They are more ambitious, more competitive. This drive to dominate appears to be an attempt to make up for inner insecurity and fear and possible weakness. They experience an acute conflict between passivity and aggressive, self assertive impulses.

The personalities of fracture patients were found to be divided into three groups—introversive, constricted, and extroverted. The first two groups showed the highest incidence of accidents. Among all the groups there is an effort to compromise between passivity and aggression with an emphasis on adaptation, self determination, independence, and day to day pleasures. The authors found that personality constriction increases with organic brain damage.

Gildea compared the personality traits of people with various psychosomatic ailments. Those with the following disorders were studied: ulcerative colitis, hypertension, hyperthyroid, rheumatoid arthritis, coronary disease, peptic ulcer, and bronchial asthma. The ulcerative colitis patients were immature and narcissistic with an excessive dependence on their mothers. They gave up easily and their attacks followed stress. The hypertensives were unable to assert themselves or to express their resentment. They manifested obsessive compulsive defenses. The hyperthyroid patients had a strong attachment to their parents or parent surrogates. They were very insecure and were unable to find outlets for their emotion. They had a strong sense of responsibility. The rheumatoid arthritics were hostile and aggressive. They often found relief by abnormal, self-sacrificing helpfulness. The women tended to be tomboys, and rejecting of the feminine role. The coronary disease patients had a great need and respect for authority. They were unremitting workers and had a great deal of "sticktoitiveness." They also had obsessive compulsive defenses. The peptic ulcer patients had strong dependent needs. The onset of the ulcer was often related to life crises. Under psychotherapy they regressed to childlike dependence. The attacks of the bronchial asthma patients were related to crying. These patients were immature and had a strong need for protection. They feared separation from and are dependent on their mothers, who in many ways reject them. Very often, separation from the mother precipitated an attack. They marry late, if at all.

Hypertension has been studied by a number of investigators. Gressel et al. examined 50 subjects with essential hypertension, 49 subjects without essential hypertension but with some kind of psychiatric illness, but not psychotic, and 44 subjects who had a chronic medical or surgical disorder, but not psychotic. Group I (essential hypertension) was divided into neurogenic hypertension and other types of hypertension. The "other" hypertensives were found to exhibit more obsessive compulsive behavior, and were more subnormally assertive than the other groups. The neurogenic hypertensives were shown to be not significantly different from the other kinds of hypertensives in their dynamics. The authors concluded that there is the possibility that the hypertensives are recurrently and frequently inhibiting their impulses to overt action. Franz Alexander, the renowned analyst, thinks that the compulsive traits represent an attempt to allay the anxiety which develops as a reaction to excessive hostile, destructive impulses. This corresponds closely with Gildea's findings of obsessive compulsive behavior and subnormal assertiveness in his hypertensive patients. He defined subnormal assertiveness as an inability to verbalize feelings even when aware of them. The patient simply "takes it" from boss, friends, wife, etc. These people are extremely pleasant and jovial and exhibit rare outbursts of hostility.

Rennie studied four cases of essential hypertension. These patients showed lifelong instability expressed in depression and anxiety. They were also perfectionistic, ambitious and were overly attentive to bodily symptoms. These people worked at top speed, had a tremendous need to succeed and had a tendency toward jealousy and suspicion. The emotional patterns appear to be those of resentment, sometimes coupled with a desire for revenge.

The most comprehensive work on the psychological aspects of coronary artery disease has been done by Friedman and his colleagues at the Mt. Zion Hospital and Medical Center in San Francisco. The initial studies of this group began back in the 1950's. In a series of articles published in the Journal of the American Medical Association, Friedman and Rosenman studied the behavior of people with blood and cardiovascular problems. In an article in the Journal of the American Medical Association three groups of men were selected solely according to their behavior pattern, which they habitually manifested in their work. The first group (Group A) of 83 were those who had an intense desire to achieve and were continually involved in competition deadlines. Eighty-three men were also chosen who had the opposite kind of behavior (Group B). The third group consisted of 46 unemployed blind men selected because they manifested a chronic state of anxiety and insecurity (Group C). Clinical coronary artery disease was seven times more frequent in group A than in group B or C. Group A men had a higher serum cholesterol, a higher frequency of arcus senilis, and a much greater smoking incidence than B, but only slightly more than C. The average ingestion of alcohol in A men was slightly higher than B, but much higher than C. The incidence of clinical artery disease in parents of A was two times that of C and one and a half times that of B. In the JAMA Rosenman et al. reported on a study of 3500 men age 39–59 by various approaches to determine what characteristics of apparently well men were of predictive importance in regard to subsequent occurrence of manifest coronary heart disease. The following physiological studies were done: total serum cholesterol, blood coagulation, and cardiovascular examination. The assessment of overt behavior pattern was made by tape recorded personal interviews requiring 30 minutes. The tape recordings consisted of two monologues, one spoken by a man, the other by a woman. The male monologue was of interest to the subjects while the female's was not. The female monologue interrupted the male monologue 12 times. The total number of separating body movements and hand clenchings were recorded on the subjects listening to the male monologue. In addition, personal, parental, and socioeconomic history, smoking habits, exercise and dietary habits were assessed. Coronary patients exhibited arcus senilis eight times as frequently as normal patients and had many more frequent deformities in their respiratory and body movements.

Other findings from this study indicate that a larger number of the coronary group were in occupations having the highest level of responsibility compared with the controls. A positive history of parental coronary heart disease was obtained from 20.4% of the coronary group as compared with 17% of the controls. Although the average daily cigarette consumption by smokers did not differ significantly between the two groups, more of the coronary group were cigarette smokers. A larger number of the coronary group than controls also had a history of high blood pressure. There was no difference in blood coagulation. Higher mean beta/alpha lipoprotein levels were observed in the coronary than controls.

As a result of their studies, Friedman and Rosenman have categorized certain personality "types" as A and B. The type A person is competitive and worried that he is behind in work, is irritable at delays in being seated on conveyances such as trains and airplanes or in being held up in traffic, is super ambitious and strives for the things held up as symbols of success in our culture—a nice house, a college education for his children, etc. This kind of person is prone to have a coronary attack.

Ginsparb and Satten reviewed 20 cases of individuals who had suffered a myocardial infarction. They surmised that the coronary represents a somatic equivalent of the suicidal impulse, results from an internalization of intense aggressive impulses and that the conflict and the guilt arising from these impulses must remain totally obscured from consciousness for the conflict to be channelized into the body. They differentiate this illness from other psychosomatic illnesses which also have the symptoms of internalized aggression in that the coronary patients have a desire to "get out of this world." In a second group, the infarction seems to have developed as the individual experienced extreme rage or anger which had exceeded the physiological limits of toleration. A third group involved those individuals who seemed to be suffering what they call "emotional drain" prior to the infarct. The primary factor here is a depletion of their inner resources and inability to "give" emotionally. These are the primary personality *causes* of coronaries and infarction. The effect is depression, the mobilization of latent conflicts and needs such as the wish to be nurtured and to regress, which regression is sometimes denied resulting in the attempt at completely unattainable physical feats. In these authors' judgment, most long term survivors are found among the reality oriented individuals—wherein the patient accepts his limitations realistically and is able to reorient his life. It has been observed that these individuals are happier after the coronary than before.

Gentry, Foster and Haney investigated the use of psychological tests in assessing the degree of affect manifested by patients in the intensive coronary care unit at Duke University Medical Center. Sixteen male and sixteen female patients admitted to the coronary care unit with a diagnosis of myocardial infarction were studied over a 5-day period on the unit. Half of the patients were classified as "deniers" and half as "Non-deniers" based on their response to the question: "Did you feel afraid, frightened or apprehensive at any time during your hospital stay thus far?" The "deniers" answered "No" to the question while "non-deniers" responded positively. In addition, a self-report of situational anxiety and depression was obtained from each patient daily and ratings of chronic anxiety and perceived health status were obtained on days 1 and 5.

The results indicated that "deniers" reported less anxiety than "non-deniers" over the five days. The non-deniers showed a significant decrease in anxiety as time went by. Non-deniers tended to experience a marked difference between current and general health status on day 1 of the study, whereas deniers did not. The estimated level of current health was lower than that of general health on day 5 with non-deniers exhibiting marked improvement in perceived current health status to day 1. In general it was found that the defense mechanism of denial is a major determinant of the level of anxiety which characterizes these coronary patients.

Cleveland and Johnson administered Rorschachs and TAT's to a group of hospitalized myocardial infarction patients and compared the results with another group of hospitalized subjects who were in a life-threatening situation and matched with the myocardial infarction patients as to age, education and socioeconomic background. They found that myocardial infarction patients were more "depressive" and "agitated" than the controls. However, this was contrary to the impression that the researchers found in interviews where the myocardial infarction patients were found to be essentially achievement oriented.

Weiss et al. examined young myocardial infarction patients and compared them with healthy subjects, using the clinical psychiatric interview. They concluded that the myocardial infarction patients had more psychiatric diseases and more sexual problems prior to the myocardial infarction than the controls.

Forssman and Lindegard studied samples carefully matched as to somatological parameters. They found that myocardial infarction patients were more "explosive" and "hysterical" than control subjects.

Ibrahim et al. compared coronary heart disease patients with "high risk" healthy subjects and with "low risk" healthy subjects ("risk" criteria were blood pressure and serum cholesterol) using the MMPI. On the basis of their results, the authors conclude that selected "coronary personality profile" (low level of manifest hostility plus elevated levels of anxiety and repression) is a result of coronary heart disease and not a cause of it.

Psychosocial factors play a considerable part in causing myocardial infarction. Various surveys in different countries have demonstrated that the incidence of myocardial infarction in young patients is related to the degree of "urbanization" of their area. The effects of treatment are the early formulation of the clinical material and focusing on denial as the primary defense, attention to the narcissistic injury created by the illness or trauma, and emphasis on the cognitive understanding of the patient of his illness. Western urbanization has been studied in Yemenite immigrants in Israel and in immigrants in the U.S.A. These studies show that both serum cholesterol and myocardial incidence rise from low levels in the native countries to high levels of western urbanized areas.

Hinkle et al. found that clerks without a college education had higher coronary artery incidences than clerks on the same level *with* a college education.

Pieper, et al studied the relation of job psychological demands and decision latitude to four coronary heart disease risk factors (cholesterol, smoking, systolic and diastolic pressure). 12,555 men in five investigations were tests in the U.S. during the period 1959–1980. Using an inputations strategy, the authors attacked measures of two job characteristics in each data base by occupation. In 19 possible tests, decision latitude was related ($p > .05$) to cholesterol and smoking in two instances in the predicted direction in the Exercise Heart Survey when controlling Types I error rate. Psychological demands were not related to any risk factors. When a meta-analysis was performed across data bases all relations were in the predicted direction except for relation of psychological demands to systolic pressure. The interaction of psychological demands and decision latitude was not related to any of the risk factors when two common forms of interaction were tested. These results indicate that the psychosocial aspects of work in particular the decision latitude of the job may be related to some cardiovascular factors.

Kasan et al. found that those with myocardial infarction had a greater tendency not to have regular vacations, to use more soporifics and analgesics habitually and to more often consider their work hectic than did age-matched patients with other diseases. Syme et al. found that people who had made four or more occupational changes had more than twice the expected prevalence of coronary heart disease. Rahe and Paasikivi, did psychosocial studies on myocardial infarction non-identical twins. In these studies the myocardial subjects proved to have experience more excessive overtime work and more life dissatisfactions than the healthy subjects.

Van der Valk and Groen found that the period prior to myocardial infarction onset was characterized by changes in many areas of the patient's life. Parkes et al discovered that the elevated mortality in men during their first months as widowers was due to myocardial infarction.

There have been a number of epidemiological studies in relation to myocardial infarction. Warwell et al. compared subjects with coronary heart disease with other controls and found that social group mobility and ethnic background were significantly discriminatory in separating the myocardial infarction group from the controls. Shekelle et al. studied a group of 1500 men, ages 40–55, over a five-year period. The subjects' socio-economic and educational discrepancy from his parents and spouse were better predictors of myocardial infarction than educational and socio-economic status alone.

Theorell and his coworkers have done a great deal of work in the Seraphimer Hospital, Karolinska Institutet in Stockholm, Sweden on the psychological and metabolic aspects of myocardial infarction and it might by pertinent to mention these in some detail.

Theorell devised a coronary heart disease questionnaire emphasizing work patterns, perceptions of being rushed in living patterns, and satisfaction or lack of satisfaction with several areas of life adjustment. He gave the questionnaire to 62 male subjects who had survived a myocardial infarction for a mean period of 18 months. The mean age of the group was 56 years. The questionnaire was also given to an equal number of healthy controls. The post-myocardial infarction patients reported a higher prevalence of excessive overtime work, of dissatisfaction with their work, and greater hostility toward others when slowed down by them than the controls. The controls reported a higher prevalence of taking work home, attendance at work and non-work related organizations, supervision of others and responsibilities at work, street relaxation, physical exercise during leisure time and dissatisfaction with their financial status.

Thus the most striking observation in this phase of the study was that the patients worked overtime excessively more often than the controls. Despite the overtime, the patients lacked satisfaction in their work which they did not consider as adding to their responsibility.

Theorell gave 54 male myocardial patients with a mean age of 61.2 years a "Schedule of Recent Experience." (Twenty-seven of these patients had no previously recognized signs or symptoms of coronary heart disease while twenty-seven did have such signs during the past three years). This SRE consisted of changes in the patient's life in the past three years, such as addition of family member, in-law troubles, troubles with boss, change to a different line of work etc. (total of 36). A "life change total" was calculated and weights assigned to each life change unit (LCU) for the past 3–4 prehospitalization years. In addition, 14 friends were utilized as a control group who had no history of infarction. The infarction patients with recent episodes of coronary heart disease or other major illness showed a significant increase in LCU totals.

There have been a number of studies assessing the effect of the environment on heart disease such as temperature extremes, noise, soft water, exposure to sulfur dioxide and carbon monoxide, and constraints imposed by the community such as non-availability of high protein foods low in saturated fats and cholesterol, and limitations on physical exercise.

Various studies have shown a clear seasonal periodicity in death rates from coronary artery disease with up to 50% more deaths occurring during the winter months. Generally the increased death rate in winter occurs in those countries (and in the U.S.) where the winters are the coldest and where there is little detectable seasonal difference. A committee of the American Heart Association considered the effect of shoveling snow, for example, and concluded that this was not of major importance. In Canada, researchers have suggested that in such places as Ontario, Australia and Denmark increased heart attacks may be caused by an increase in respiratory ailments having a secondary effect on the heart. Insofar as heat is concerned, a report from Finland states that in 1970 there were 67 deaths among people taking sauna baths. On a community basis in St. Louis in 1966 there were over 300 deaths in six days during a heat wave, one-third of these attributed to atherosclerotic heart disease.

The effect of noise is uncertain and is thought to be interwoven with the whole problem of stress. Similarly, there is little evidence that exposure to ionizing radiation has increased death from heart disease (the Hiroshima survivors showed no excess of heart disease). This is particularly significant in medicine because the use of microwaves is becoming more important in medical practice.

With the problem of air pollution in the United States becoming more acute, air pollution episodes associated with high levels of sulfur dioxide (as have occurred in London and Danora) have been associated with a marked increase in deaths from atherosclerotic heart disease. However, in the main these deaths were limited to those persons with a chronic pre-existent cardio-pulmonary disease. Experimental animals that were fed cholesterol and exposed to small levels of carbon monoxide do develop atherosclerosis. It is entirely possible that this may be the reason why long-term cigarette smokers develop atherosclerosis. However, there is no conclusive proof that garage workers or people who work in enclosed tunnels show an increased risk of death from heart disease, although municipal sanitation workers in New York City, exposed to the exhaust fumes of their vehicles did have an increased death rate from coronary artery disease. It might be that driving in an automobile with closed windows in city traffic and smoking large numbers of cigarettes, may account for the coronary artery disease deaths in the larger cities.

It is thought that hard water somehow exerts a protective influence against heart disease, although the exact mechanism is not known. For example, in Monroe County, Florida (Florida Keys) the introduction of hard water from the mainland was associated with a marked drop in deaths resulting from heart disease. It may be that somehow calcium is the protective influence.

Of great importance are the prevailing living patterns within a community or group of people. On a national basis, visits to supermarkets or grocery stores show that there is little or any labeling of those items high in cholesterol or saturated fats which might be injurious to health or might precipitate cardiac difficulty. According to a recent study, the Seven Day Adventists who do not smoke, have a life expectancy in California (where the study was done) that is six years longer for males than males in the general population.

ADDITIONAL CAUSES

In recent years there has been great emphasis on diet in relation to various kinds of heart disease with particular focus on the intake of saturated and unsaturated fats. While it is not the intent or function of this work to expound either on the physiological, pathological, or nutritional etiology of cardiac disease, it might be of interest to inspect some further studies in this area also done by Friedman and Rosenman. In one study they obtained a detailed dietary history of 46 women and their husbands, belonging to an upper socio-economic stratum. No significant difference was found in the caloric or percentage of fat intake for each sex when corrected for difference in surface area. A critical review of various data relating to the relative immunity of the American woman to clinical coronary artery disease suggests that this immunity cannot be due entirely to some endocrine induced protection against the supposed atherogenic properties of a high fat diet. The authors conclude that probably greater stress in males causes coronary artery disease.*

The list of factors associated with the development of heart disease has grown in recent years. These include lack of physical activity, smoking, and a low concentration of certain dissolved minerals in the water supply. More recently there has been a controversy about the etiology of heart disease due to ingestion of large amounts of coffee. In December, 1972, Jick, Slone et al. observed an association between heavy coffee drinking and myocardial infarction at the Boston Collaborative Drug Surveillance Program of Boston University Medical Center. They estimated that the risk of developing myocardial infarction is about twice as great for heavy coffee drinkers as it is for those who drink no coffee at all. This conclusion was confirmed in August 1973 in a second large study by this group. In their first report the researchers compared 276 myocardial patients from eight hospitals in the United States, Canada, New Zealand and Israel with 1104 closely matched control patients with other diseases. In the second study, they compared 440 white, middle-aged (age 40–69) subjects from 24 Boston area hospitals with a matched control series of 12,319 patients hospitalized with other diseases. In both studies, they found patients who drank 1–5 cups of coffee daily ran an approximately 50% greater risk of developing myocardial infarction than those who drank no coffee; patients who drank six cups daily or more ran about 110% greater risk. However, the investigators found no association between heavy coffee drinking and such closely related infarction progenitors as obesity, hypertension, and coronary insufficiency. The group also found a slight and negative correlation of coffee drinking with cigarette smoking, but there was only a slightly increased risk of infarction associated with smoking and a lesser overall risk associated with smoking than with coffee. Jick says this is consistent with previously published reports that smoking engenders the greatest risk of heart disease among individuals who are otherwise healthy, and the risk associated with smoking decreases as the risk of other factors increases.

Other investigators have obtained other results as to the relation of coffee drinking and heart disease. In the Framingham, Massachusetts Heart Disease Epidemiology Study, Kannell and Dawber, under the auspices of the National Institute of Health, monitored more than 5100 adult residents of Framingham over a 20-year period in an attempt to detect dietary, environmental, physiological and personality traits that

---

*It is now thought that rennin, a hormone secreted by the juxta glomerular cells of the kidney is secreted in the blood and reacts with the blood plasma to cause the formation of angiotensin which in turn produces hypertension.

increase the risk of heart disease. Their results indicate that there is no relationship between drinking coffee and heart disease.

Heyden of the Duke University Medical Center in Durham, North Carolina monitored more than 2500 results of Eruns County, Georgia for five years. He also found that there was no evidence that heart disease of any type is more frequent among those who drink large amounts of coffee.

Paul of the Northwestern University Medical School of Chicago monitored the health of more than 1700 middle-aged men in Chicago for three years. He reported an increased incidence of heart disease among those subjects who consumed large amounts of coffee. Five years later, however, he reported that a major portion of the association between coffee and heart disease could be attributed to an association between smoking and heart disease, since heavy smokers are generally also heavy coffee drinkers and vice versa. Paradoxically he also found that the mortality rate among both smoking and non-smoking myocardial infarction victims was lower for coffee drinkers than for non-drinkers and that smokers who are heavy coffee drinkers run less risk of developing myocardial infarctions than smokers who are non-drinkers.

There have been a number of smaller studies which have produced contradictory results. For example, Wilhelmin and Tribben in Sweden have monitored the health of 835 residents of Gothenburg since 1963 (10 years). They found no association between coffee drinking and heart disease. Thiel and his associates at the University of Oklahoma School of Medicine compared 50 subjects with an equal number of closely matched controls and found a significantly increased consumption of fluids including coffee among myocardial infarction patients. Other small scale studies have generally revealed no link between coffee consumption and heart disease, although nearly all investigators have noted strong correlations between coffee drinking and smoking, and between smoking and heart disease.

In addition to diet, other risk factors have been studied. An interesting continuing study being conducted by Wilmore at the University of California Medical Center in San Francisco, California investigated whether the effect of the risk factor can be cancelled by a change in the person's life style such as a carefully programmed exercise regimen. The interesting element of this study is that the subjects are 95 schoolboys ranging in age from 8–12 years, who come from two public schools in Davis, California. They are healthy, well-fed, relatively affluent and far above average compared with the national norms for endurance and stamina. In addition to being weighted regularly, measurements are taken of body fat, cholesterol, and EKG's. The are also given a battery of endurance tests. Of the 95, 36 were on the borderline of obesity while 12 were obese; there was a significantly high cholesterol level in eight youngsters; 32 had a family history of heart attack under age 60; and abnormal EKG's were taken at rest for two boys and after exercise in three. The boys from one of the Davis schools have been given a special exercise program while the boys from the other program have continued with their normal school physical education activities. The results of this study have not yet been published.

PATIENTS, QUESTIONNAIRE AND RESULTS

THE PATIENTS

The patients in the cardiac project were both hospitalized and ambulatory, and all were afflicted with cardiac disease in the following categories:

I. Arteriosclerotic Heart Disease—patients with angina pectoris, acute myocardial infarction and coronary artery disease.

II. Hypertensive Vascular Disease—patients with essential hypertension, renal hypertension, malignant hypertension and endocrine disturbances.

III. Disturbances of Conduction—patients with S.A. or A.V. block.

IV. Valvular Disease—patients with mitral stenosis, mitral insufficiency, aortic insufficiency, tricuspid stenosis and tricuspid insufficiency.

Diagnosis was made by the cardiologist in the hospital or clinic or if a private patient, by the patient's personal physician. See Table I for a summary of the patients and their diagnosis.

QUESTIONNAIRE[1]

The questionnaire was designed to assess various psychological aspects of the patient's disease, but other areas also were explored. In addition to identifying data such as age, sex, diagnosis, medication, marital status, data symptoms first noticed and what they were, the life change unit (LCU) self concept was explored. Such information as kinds of psychological disturbance at time of occurrence of symptoms, i.e., stress, loss of someone close before or after symptoms, difficulty with career or money, were assessed. Various other psychosomatic manifestations such as headache, enuresis, tics, were also assessed both during childhood and adulthood. Subjective estimates of psychological variables such as

---

[1]see appendix for full questionnaire.

TABLE 1
DIAGNOSES

N-124	
*ARTERIOSCLEROTIC HEART DISEASE**	
ASHD (%)	66
Myocardial infarction (%)	26
Myocardial insufficiency (%)	03
Angina (%)	10
N-87	
HYPERTENSIVE CARDIOVASCULAR DISEASE	
Hypertention (%)	100
N-72	
*VALVULAR**	
Aortic insufficiency (%)	57
Rheumatic heart disease (%)	22
Valve replacement (%)	14
Mitral Stenosis (%)	07
Subacute bacterial endocarditis (%)	07
N-56	
*DISTURBANCE OF CONDUCTION**	
Heart block or complete heart block (%)	50
Congestive heart failure (%)	33
Bilateral branch block (%)	17
Disturbance of conduction (%)	17

*The total is more than 100% since some patients had more than one diagnosis.

ambition, persistence, dependency, expression in grief and rage, conformity were obtained. Frequency and type of nocturnal dreams and daydreams were also assessed. Familial information such as personality of parents, which parent was dominant in the home, family attitude toward heart disease, incidence of psychosomatic ailments in family were collected. A fairly detailed work history on each patient was obtained including how well the patient got along with employees, employers and other superiors. Strength of religious belief was obtained for each patient. Elements tangential to psychological variables were obtained from each patient such as alcohol ingestion, smoking, use of drugs, diet, and exercise previous to and after symptoms were assessed.[2] Finally, satisfaction with current treatment was asked of each patient.

ANALYSIS OF QUESTIONNAIRE

The questionnaire was analyzed for information both *within* each cardiac group and *between* cardiac groups. Inasmuch as numbers are meaningless, the *percentages* in each category of heart disease were computed.

ARTERIOSCLEROTIC HEART DISEASE

Here the number of subjects was slightly in favor of males—59% males to 41% females. The average age of each sex was almost exactly the same—58.65 years for males and 58.92 years for females. Interestingly, the largest percentage was widowed and the next largest were married. Forty-five percent had some relatives with heart disease, indicating that to some extent this type of heart disease has a familial diathesis. Of this group with someone in the family having heart disease, in the largest number (18%) the father was afflicted, with the next largest the mother (15%). Eighty-five percent of this group had their heart disease for over two years and only 15% had the disease under 2 years. Only a small fraction of those with this kind of heart disease (17%) had lost someone close to them at the time of the appearance of symptoms, and only 10% of this group said they had financial problems at the time of the appearance of symptoms. The conception of how disabled they were due to this type of heart disease ranged from moderately (52%) to severely disabled (45%) with only 3% stating that they were not disabled at all. A total of 97% of this group thought they were either moderately or totally disabled. As one might expect, the reaction of relatives to the patient's illness was greatest—

[2]At the time the heart patients were being questioned, coffee drinking was not thought to have any influence on the etiology of heart disease.

38% of the relatives greatly upset by the appearance of the disease as against 24% of friends and 16% of acquaintances being greatly upset. In both acquaintances and friends the largest group was moderately upset and a goodly percentage of the relatives moderately upset. Another interesting finding in this type of heart disease is that a goodly number, 84%, had lost some close relatives by death just previous to the symptoms, spread rather evenly by husband (16%), wife (14%), father (14%), brother (14%), and mother (10%). This suggests that loss of a close relative may precipitate an attack of this type of heart disease. Insofar as other psychosomatic ailments having hysterical components are concerned, either as a child or adult, headaches, temper tantrums, tremors, and heart pains do seem to have some relationship to this kind of heart disease—35% had headaches as a child (16% one per week and 19% one per month); 30% had headaches as an adult (15% very often—one per day and 15% one every three days) and 38% one per month. Only a small percentage had tremors as a child but 27% had tremors either one per week or one per month as an adult (15% one per week and 12% one per month). Twenty-seven percent had temper tantrums either one per week or one per month as a child (12% one per week and 15% one per month) while 20% admitted to temper tantrums once every three days, one per week or one per month (4% once every three days, 4% once every week and 12% once a month). Sixteen percent said they had cardiac pain as a child either once a week or once a month (4% once a week and 12% once a month), while as might be expected, 69% said they currently had heart pains once a month or more (15% every day; 15% one every three days; 27% one every week and 12% once a month). Practically none of these patients admitted to having tics, convulsions, enuresis, or to having stuttered, bitten their nails or sucked their thumb either as a child or adult.

RESULTS OF HYPERTENSIVE VASCULAR DISEASE

These patients were of a single, middle aged, "established" religious group where heart disease in the family seemed to be no factor, although a large number had lost their mother (not by heart disease) just previous to symptoms. They perceived themselves as either moderately or severely disabled because of their heart disease. Headaches were predominant as an hysterical psychosomatic symptom both as a child and adult, with tremors also present to some extent as a child. Temper tantrums were also present as a child. A large majority of these patients got angry easily and also withdrew from difficult situations. In general, they had good self concept and got along with all members of the family while growing up.

They had an excellent work record, with an average of 14 years on the job, and according to their own assertions got along with their bosses and colleagues. Emotional upset brought about an exacerbation of symptoms.

VALVULAR DISEASE

There were 57% males and 43% females in this group. The average age of the males was 43.13 years and the average age of the females 40.5 years. Most of these patients were separated (36%), while 29% were married, 14% divorced, 14% single, and 7% widowed. Half of these patients had someone else in the family with heart disease: mother—22%; brother—11%; father—6%; sister—6%; wife—6%. Seventy-one percent had their ailment over 2 years, and 29% under 2 years. Twenty-one percent had difficulty with money just previous to their heart disease. Another 21% had lost someone close to them just previous to their heart disease. Seventy-one percent thought they were moderately disabled due to their heart disease, 14% thought they were severely disabled, and 15% not at all disable. Forty-six percent of the relatives were moderately upset about the patient's heart problem, 23% were indifferent, 23% greatly upset, and 8% were mildly upset. Approximately the same figures were true of friends; 43% were moderately upset, 21% indifferent, 21% greatly upset, 7% mildly upset, and 7% had other reactions. Twenty-seven percent of the acquaintances were either greatly or moderately upset, 18% indifferent, and 9% other reactions. Twenty-nine percent of these patients lost their mother just previous to symptoms, while 17% lost a husband, 11% a wife, and 6% a father, sister or aunt. Twenty-four percent had not lost anyone just prior to symptoms.

Headaches and temper tantrums were the only two psychosomatic variables with any "significant" incidence in this group either as a child or adult. Twenty-one percent had headaches; quite often (14%) moderately often (7%); while 21% had headaches hardly ever as a child. The occurrence of headaches as an adult was somewhat greater, with 21% having them quite often and 14% moderately often. Twenty-one percent had temper tantrums as a child; quite often (7%); moderately often (14%). But as an adult none had temper tantrums either very often or quite often, and only 7% had temper tantrums moderately often. In all the other variables, the incidence was negligible, although again as might be expected, 14% had heart pains quite often, and 43% had heart pains moderately often as an adult. Thirty-one percent of this group said they got angry easily, and 43% said they withdrew from difficult situations.

A large majority of these patients said they were ambitious (71%), persistent (92%), in good control of themselves (93%), moody (71%) clean (100%), independent (69%), and adequate (86%). As for expressions of emotions, 54% were *unable* to express grief, all were able to express joy, 75% able to express rage, and all able to express other emotions. Seventy-seven percent were able to conform to everyday mores. All of these patients dreamed at one time or another, with 8% dreaming practically every night, 25% once every few nights, and 8% one night per week; 59% dreamed less than one night per week; eighty-four percent had dreams which were either very clear (42%) or moderately clear (42%). Most (78%) of these patients dreamed less than half the night. Thirty-nine percent of this group had daydreams, with 80% daydreaming either practically every day (20%) or once every few days (60%). Half had very clear daydreams and half moderately clear. A large number (25%) daydreamed about money, with 13% daydreaming about vacations or work, and 49% about other things. Ninety-two percent of these patients got along well (85%) or very well (7%) with their mother. Seventy percent got along very well (10%) or well (60%) with their father. None got along very well with their siblings but 77% got along well. In most of the families of these patients (65%), the father was the disciplinarian, while in the remainder the mother was the disciplinarian (35%). Fifty percent of the families of this group saw the patient's heart disease either as a serious problem or were sympathetic (25%), 17% were indifferent, 8% accepted the situation, and 25% didn't know how their families felt about the heart disease. Thirty-three percent of these patients had someone in the family with some kind of psychosomatic ailment, and of this group none was the mother or father; all the ailments occurred in some other relatives. Average stay on the job was 4.77 years ranging from 2 months to 11 years. Seventy-three percent said they enjoyed their work and all said they got along with their boss and colleagues in their job just previous to their heart attack and previous jobs.

Insofar as religion was concerned, this group had about an equal spread among all categories; 31% were extremely religious, 23% moderately religious, 23% went to place of worship sometimes, and 23% never.

Seventy-seven percent said they felt good about the doctor examining them, while 23% said it didn't bother them. All were satisfied with the treatment they were getting. Fifty-four percent said that their symptoms increased when they got emotionally upset, and 54% said that their symptoms increased when they exercised. Only 15% said that their symptoms increased under certain weather conditions (50% hot weather, 50% cold weather), and 31% during certain seasons (75% summer, 25% winter.)

RESULTS OF VALVULAR GROUP

These patients were also a middle aged "establishment" group but considerably younger than the arteriosclerotic or hypertensive groups. Their heart disease was chronic (over two years). They thought their disease was either moderately or severely disabling. The majority of relatives or friends were moderately or greatly upset due to their heart disease. A large number lost their mother just previous to the appearance of symptoms. Headaches and temper tantrums were two hysterical psychosomatic symptoms which were present in these patients both as a child and adult. All of them reported a good self concept. All seemed to get along with their mother and father in their formative years, and in this group the father was the disciplinarian. Their work history was fairly good but not as good as the arteriosclerotics and hypertensives. All claimed to have gotten along well with colleagues and bosses on the job. A majority said their symptoms increased when they were emotionally upset.

DISTURBANCE OF CONDUCTION

In this group, 67% were males and 33% females. The average age of the males was 60 years; females 62.5 years. Fifty percent of these patients were single, while 17% were divorced, 17% married, and 16% separated, while none were widowed. Forty-three percent of these patients had someone in the family with heart disease, equally divided among father, brother, grandfather, and son. Eighty percent had their affliction over 2 years, and 20% under 2 years. Seventeen percent had lost someone close to them just before their symptoms, while 34% had money problems just previous to their symptoms. Fifty percent of these patients thought they were moderately disabled, while 33% thought they were severely disabled, and 17% not at all disabled (83% moderately or severely disabled). Of their relatives, friends, and acquaintances, 67% of the relatives were moderately upset by the patients' heart ailment, while 33% were greatly upset; 80% of the friends were moderately upset, while 20% of the friends were greatly upset; the same figures were true of acquaintances. Of those who had lost someone close just before symptoms, they were divided equally (17% among father, mother, husband, and son). Of the psychosomatic ailments assessed, symptomatology as a child was noticeably absent, except for temper tantrums and heart pains. However, a large number of these patients did have symptomatology of headaches, tremors, and surprisingly enough enuresis, temper tantrums, and heart pains. Sixty-seven percent of these patients had temper tantrums moderately often as a child, while 17% had heart pains very often as a child.

However, 20% had headaches quite often, or moderately often (40%) as an adult; 17% had tremors either very often or moderately often 17%). Seventeen percent were enuretic moderately often as an adult. Seventeen percent currently had heart pains moderately often, 33% of these patients got angry easily, while half withdrew from difficult situations and half did not. All claimed to be ambitious and persistent, while 84% said they were in good control of themselves. Half said they were moody, while half said they were not. All thought they were clean. Sixty-seven percent said that they were independent and all thought they were adequate. Sixty-seven percent said that they were able to express grief, 83% able to express joy, 33% able to express rage, and 60% able to express other emotions. All said they conformed to everyday mores.

All of these patients said they dreamed, with 33% dreaming practically every night, 33% once every few nights, and 17% one night every few weeks. Eighty-four percent of these patients' dreams were either very clear or moderately clear. Most of them dreamed less than half the night (67%); 33% daydreamed, while 67% did not. Of the 33%, half daydreamed practically every day, while half daydreamed less than one day per week. All of them had very clear daydreams. Of those that did daydream, half daydreamed about accomplishments, and half about discipline. Eighty percent of these patients got along very well (20%), or well (60%) with their mother while 75% got along with their father, and 25% only fair. Fifty percent got along well with their sibs; 25% fair; and 25% poorly. In 50% of the cases, the mother was the disciplinarian; 33% the father; 17% somebody else. In 33% of the group, the patients didn't know how their family felt about their heart disease; 33% were in some other category than that assessed by the questionnaire. In 17% the family was indifferent, and in 17% the family thought it was a serious problem. Thirty-three percent had someone in the family with psychosomatic ailments, with 33% the mother, and 67% some other members of the family. The average length on the job of this group was 2 years. Considering that the average age for males was 60 years and 62.5 years for females, this was really short duration of job tenure.

Fewer of these patients (80%) said they got along with their boss well than the other types of heart patients. The same holds true as to enjoying their job (80%) and getting along with others on the job (75%). The percentage are even lower for past work with 50% getting along well with their boss and 50% either fair or badly; 50% got along well with others in their past work and 50% fairly well.

The majority of these patients were moderately religious (60%), while 40% said they rarely went to a place of worship.

Fifty percent said that they feel good about the doctor examining them, while 50% said it doesn't bother them. All were satisfied with the treatment they were getting. Eighty-three percent said that their symptoms were increased when they were emotionally upset, half said their symptoms increased when they exercised, one-third said their symptoms increased under certain weather conditions (cold 33%, damp 33%, and heat 34%). One-third said their symptoms increase during a certain season (1/3 Spring, 1/3 Winter, and 1/3 Summer). One-third said their symptoms increased at other times (50% when tired, and 50% when they argued with their children).

RESULTS OF DISTURBANCE OF CONDUCTION

This group of patients had the highest average age of all the patients. However, they were also an "establishment" group, most of whom were single. Their affliction was chronic and there seems to be a familial diathesis in their disease. The majority thought they were either seriously or moderately disabled. Relatives, friends, and acquaintances were quite upset by their heart ailment. Thus, it appears that this kind of cardiac disease (disturbance of conduction) does upset those surrounding the patient. Headaches, tremors, and temper tantrums were currently present and a goodly number had temper tantrums as a child. Insofar as self concept is concerned, the positive self concept expressed by other cardiac patients was not as unanimous in this group. The chief difference in the variables was in moodiness where half said they were moody and 37% said they were dependent. Their job tenure was relatively short. Of all the cardiac patients, this group got along less well with their bosses and colleagues than the others. A goodly number said their symptoms increased under emotional stress.

COMPARISONS OF VARIOUS KINDS OF HEART DISEASE

Since this was an older set of patients, all groups were "establishment" and conformed to current mores. Their heart affliction was chronic. The oldest group included those who suffered from disturbance of conduction, and in descending chronological order: arteriosclerotic heart disease, hypertensive vascular disease, and valvular disease. The marital state of these patients is an interesting phenomenon, being widely divergent. The hypertensive and disturbances of conduction groups were primarily single, the arteriosclerotic primarily widowed, and the valvular separated. Just why this is so is not clear, since it might be postulated that the stresses of married life might precipitate almost any kind of heart disease, yet in none of these groups was the married state predominant. It may be that the precipitants are independent of the marital state. The arteriosclerotic group had a definite familial diathesis, while the valvular and disturbance of conduction groups have a possible familial diathesis. Loss of someone, particularly the mother, just previous to symptoms was characteristic of the arteriosclerotic hypertensive, and valvular but not the disturbance of conduction group. Temper tantrums and tremor are a surprising set of syndromes both as a child and adult in the arteriosclerotic heart patients, and headaches in the hypertensive patients, while headaches and temper tantrums were evidenced in the valvular group; headache, tremor and temper tantrums were present in the disturbance of conduction group. Practically all of the heart patients in each group thought themselves moderately disabled. In each group, except for disturbance of conduction, the patients had a universally high regard for themselves according to their self reports. All got along well with members of their family while they were growing up. Disciplinarian in the family varied with the mother in the arteriosclerotic, father in hypertensives and split evenly between mother and father in the other two groups. In none of these patients were psychosomatic present to any extent in relatives. The hypertensives were the only group that got angry easily and withdrew from difficult situations. All patients, according to their subjective reports, had a good work history (previous to heart condition) getting along with bosses and colleagues. Length on the job varied from a mean of 2 years in the disturbance of conduction group, to 14 years in the hypertensive group. Emotional upset caused an exacerbation of symptoms with a majority of all patients except the arteriosclerotic.

ALCOHOL, SMOKING, DRUGS, EXERCISE AND FATTY FOODS

Because of the controversy about and importance of these elements in relation to heart disease, they will be considered separately in each category of heart disease, and also as a whole.

ARTERIOSCLEROTIC HEART DISEASE

In this group, 19% imbibed alcohol either more than once a week or once a week (22%) previous to this heart condition, while 44% imbibed alcohol less than once per week, with 15% never touching alcohol. In relation to the general population and the incidence of inebriation, this is a considerable number of people with arteriosclerotic heart disease who imbibed alcohol either often or very often. Thirty-three percent smoked more than one pack of cigarettes a day, while 44% moderately (38%), 41% mildly, and 4% not at all previous to their heart attack. Eighteen percent ate fatty foods either a great deal, or moderately (35%), 31% small amounts, and 14% never ate fatty foods.

In all the different kinds of heart disease, ingestion of fatty foods seem to be a significant eating pattern in patients just previous to their heart disease. Ingestion in either moderate or large amounts of alcohol previous to their heart attack seems to be a factor in *arteriosclerotic heart disease* and *valvular disease*, but not in the other. In only those patients with valvular disease does smoking appear to be a factor. Since practically all of these patients exercised a good deal previous to their heart attack, it could not be ascertained whether lack of exercise might have an influence on the etiology of any specific kind of heart disease. Drugs taken previous to the affliction seems to have no influence whatsoever.

EXPERIMENTAL DESIGN

A cluster analysis is a method of objectively grouping together entities on the basis of their similarities or differences. When the entities compared are variables such as mental abilities or personality traits, the procedure is called "cluster analysis of variables" or simply "V analysis." It was previously labelled "factor analysis," a term still used, though strictly speaking it refers only to the mathematical procedures of analyses called "factoring." The term cluster analysis applies equally well to entities that are objects such as persons. The procedure of grouping together objects that have similar patterns or characteristics is known as cluster analysis of objects or simply "O analysis." This cluster analysis is one of the procedures used in nearly all fields of human thought and scientific study. The specific program in this cluster analysis is the BC TRY SYSTEM of cluster and factor analysis. THE BC TRY SYSTEM was developed by the late Professor Robert Tryon, Professor of Psychology at the University of California in Berkeley. It includes programs such as cluster analyses on as many as 2,000 variables (known as the BIGN analysis). In a cluster analysis, the procedure consists essentially of an input mechanism, control data cards, the system tape containing the program which perform the factor or cluster analysis and the executive program putting these components into operation, and data storage tape used for further analysis. The monitor output tapes contain all printed and punched output available to the user.

In the BC TRY SYSTEM as applied to this project, the variables which cluster together to form 3 factors were delineated. Then those heart disease patients which clustered on these factors were ascertained. Finally the *groups* of cardiac patients which clustered on each factor were also ascertained. In this way I could ascertain the personality variables for each group of cardiac patients.

The variables in the BC TRY program were essentially scales of various personality tests.* These were as follows:

Test I—Multiple Affect Check List—Today Form

This instrument was chosen because it is relatively short and is not taxing on the energy and resources of the subject. Since heart patients were being tested, the author did not think it feasible to use instruments like the MMPI which might tax the resources of these patients. The test consists of 132 adjectives measuring "affect traits" in which the examinee is asked to check those adjectives describing how he feels the day he takes the test and also how he feels in general. The best definition of the scales is embodied in some of the items in them.

Variable #1

A. Anxiety—

	[x]afraid	desperate	[x]fearful
[x]frightened	[x]nervous	[x]panicky	[x]shaky
[x]tense	terrified	[x]upset	[x]worrying

Variable #2

B. Depression—

destroyed	[x]discouraged	[x]forlorn	[x]gloomy
[x]hopeless	[x]lonely	[x]lost	[x]low
[x]miserable	[x]rejected	sad	[x]suffering
[x]sunk	[x]terrible	[x]tormented	[x]wilted

Variable #3

C. Hostility—

[x]disagreeable	[x]angry	bitter	[x]cruel
discontented	disgusted	enraged	furious
irritated	[x]mad	mean	offended
outraged	stormy	vexed	unsociable

*X refers to items showing high correlation with full test.

---

*The reader can obtain information concerning the tests used in this study from the psychological literature.

Variable #4

Test II—Cardiac Adjustment Scale

This is a test of 160 items which determines readiness of cardiacs for safe return to work.

Test III—Tennessee Self Concept Scale (Counseling Form)

This is an instrument which measures self concept. The individual's concept of himself has been demonstrated to be highly influential in determining his behavior and is also related to his general personality and state of mental health. The total scale consists of 100 self descriptive statements which the subject uses to portray his own picture of himself. Various scores or areas of self concept are delineated. Those used in this study are as follows:

Variable #5

1. Self Criticism Score (SC): High scores indicates a normal openness and capacity for self criticism.

Variable #6

2. Total P Score: Persons with high scores tend to like themselves, feel they are persons of value and worth and have confidence in themselves.

Variable #7

3. Row 1 P Score—Identity: These are "what I am" items. Here the individual is describing his basic identity—what he is as he sees himself.

Variable #8

4. Row 2 P Score—Self Satisfaction: This score reflects the level of self satisfaction or self acceptance. High scores indicate great self satisfaction and great self acceptance.

Variable #9

5. Row 3 P Score—Behavior: This score measures the individual's perception of his own behavior in the way he functions.

Variable #10

6. Column A—Physical Self: Here the individual is presenting his view of his body, his state of health, his physical appearance, skills and sexuality. High scores indicate positive attitudes toward these areas.

Variable #11

7. Column B—Moral Ethical Self: This score describes the self from a moral-ethical frame of reference—moral worth, relationship to God, feelings of being a "good" or "bad" person and satisfaction with one's religion or lack of it. High scores indicate perception of self as positive in the moral-ethical area.

Variable #12

8. Column C—Personal Self: This score reflects the individual's sense of personal worth, his feeling of adequacy as a person and his evaluation of his personality apart from his body or relationship to others. High scores indicate a good sense of personal worth.

Variable #13

9. Column D—Family Self: This score reflects one's feeling of adequacy, worth and value as a family member. High scores indicate perception of self as a good family member.

Variable #14

10. Column E—Social Self: This reflects the person's sense of adequacy and worth in his social interaction with other people in general. High scores indicate high sense of worth in this area.

Variable #15

11. Total V—Total Variability: This measures the amount of variability or inconsistency from one area of self perception to the other. High scores indicate the subject is so variable from one area to another as to reflect little unity or integration.

Variable #16

12. Column Total V: This score summarizes the variations within columns.

Variable #17

13. Row Total V: This score is the sum of the variations across the rows.

Variable #18

14. Distribution Score D: This score measures the degree of certainty as to the way the subject sees himself. High scores mean that the subject is very definite and certain in what he says about himself.

Test IV—Holtzman Ink Blot Test:

This is an ink blot test somewhat similar to the Rorschach which delineates personality but is more easily quantifiable. There are 23 "variables" or scores which are obtained. In this study 15 of the 23 were used and each one become a subsequent variable for the cluster analysis.

The Holtzman scores which were employed are as follows:

Variable #19

1. Space—S: Indicative of oppositional tendencies, resistance or hostility.

Variable #20

2. Color—C: Lack of achromatic or chromatic color is an indication of psychoneurotic tendencies and responsiveness to influences of the environment.

Variable #21

3. Shading—Sh: Excess shading is an indication of intellectualized anxiety, sensitivity and a capacity for warm interpersonal relations.

Variable #22

4. Movement—M: This is an indication of ego strength, developmental maturity and imaginative processes. In excess, high Ms indicate fantasy and thought disorder processes.

Variable #23

5. Pathognomic Verbalization—V: This is an indication of psychotic thought processes.

Variable #24

6. Integration—I: This is an indicator of bizarre ideation. It is also an indicator of the degree of seeking relationship between the separate fact of experience and achieving an organized view of the world.

Variable #25

7. Human—H: This is an indicator of a rich inner life, ability to empathize and conscious control over own feelings and impulses.

Variable #26

8. Animal—A: Large number of animal responses indicate aggression and the coming to the fore of basic instincts.

Variable #27

9. Anatomy—At: This indicates a narcissistic preoccupation with self and in some instances, depending on the anatomical responses, schizophrenic tendencies.

Variable #28

10. Sex—Sx (Sex responses): In some cases, a large number of sex responses is also an indicator of pathological thinking.

Variable #29

11. Abstract—Ab: This is an indication of over-intellectualization, and depending upon the relationship with other variables, high scores indicate significant psychopathology.

Variable #30

12. Anxiety—AX: Here anxiety indicates such emotions as fear, sorrow, and pity.

Variable #31

13. Hostility—Hs: Indicates tendencies which are destructive or potentially destructive toward man.

Variable #32

14. Balance—B: This is also an indication of psychotic ideation.

Variable #33

15. Popular—P: This is an indication of ties to reality. High scores indicate good ties to reality.

EXPERIMENTAL RESULTS

Three factors were extracted from the data as a result of the cluster analysis. The definitions of these factors are as follows:

Factor I

*Test and Scale**	*Definition*
1. Total I—Tennessee Self Concept Scale:	Self Worth in General
2. R2-Tennessee Self Concept Scale:	Self Satisfaction and Self Acceptance

3. R3—Tennessee Self Concept Scale:	Perception of Own Behavior
4. CA—Tennessee Self Concept Scale:	Perception of physical self including body, state of health, physical appearance and sexuality.
5. CB—Tennessee Self Concept Scale:	Perception of Moral and Ethical self.
6. CC—Tennessee Self Concept Scale:	Perception of personal worth including feeling of adequacy as a person and evaluation of his personality
7. CD—Tennessee Self Concept Scale:	Perception of social self including adequacy and worth in his social interaction with other people in general.

This factor was tentatively named physical, moral, social, personal self concept and self worth, self acceptance and self satisfaction in general.

Factor II

1. Pathognomic Verbalization—Holtzman:	Psychotic Thought
2. Sex—Holtzman:	Sexual Dysfunction and Pathological Thinking
3. Abstract—Holtzman:	Over intellectualization
4. Anxiety—Holtzman:	Evidence of fear and sorrow

Factor III

This factor encompassed the 3 scales of the Multiple Affect Check List and two of the Holtzman—movement and human. The galaxy of words that would describe this factor would be fearful, discouraged and angry with possible thought disorder. This factor is indicative of psychopathology but to a much lesser extent than Factor II.

In order to determine the "strength" of each cardiac group on each factor, the mean T scores were computed on each factor for each cardiac group. Results are shown on the accompanying graph (Figure I).

MIGRAINE

Grimes in 1931 found that of 15,000 individuals examined in general practice with reference to migraine, 1,200 or 8% were afflicted. Lennox found an incidence of 5.4% of migraine among 1,000 medical students

Figure 1. T-SCORES FOR EACH CARDIAC GROUP ON EACH FACTOR

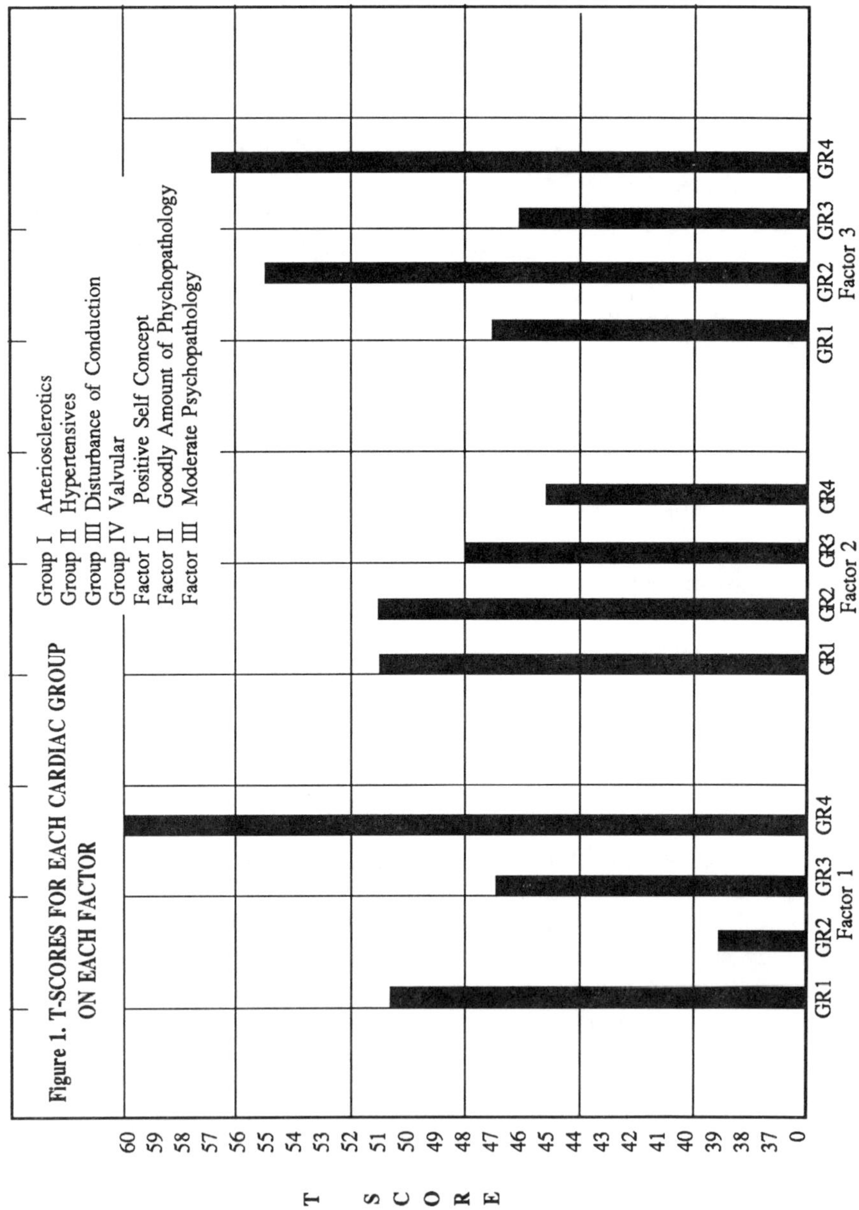

Scores of various cardiac groups insofar as psychopathology is concerned.

and nurses. In his series of migraine patients 61% were able to recall that some relative also had attacks of "sick headache."

Some of the most eminent and outstanding people in history had migraine attacks. Caesar, Paul, Kant, and Freud all were attacked by this scourge, and its pathogenesis puzzled Hippocrates.

Headache is undoubtedly the most common symptomatology of migraine, but it is not the only one. A variety of different syndromes is universally recognized within the migraine syndrome. Such symptomatology as nausea, vomiting, diarrhea, fever, abdominal pain, and even emotional concomitants such as mood changes, etc., are all part of the migraine complex. When the headache predominates, the syndrome is called common migraine; when the other symptoms predominate, it is called migraine equivalents.

In the migraine equivalents, there is periodic headache, usually unilateral in onset, but which later may become generalized. Accompanying the headache are irritability and nausea with vomiting, constipation and diarrhea. Very often the attacks are preceded by hemianopsia, unilateral paresthesias and speech abnormalities. The headache is described by the patient as a violent, throbbing pain in one temple, but becomes diffused later on in the attack. The sites of the headache are usually temporal, supraorbital, frontal, retrobulbar, parietal, postauricular and occipital. However, they may occur in the molar region, in the upper and lower teeth, at the base of the nose, in the median wall of the orbit, in the region of the common carotid artery, and sometimes as far down as the top of the tip of the shoulder. The throbbing is usually synchronized with arterial pulsation; the intensity of the throbbing is usually proportional to the increased amplitude of the various arterial pulses. The pain may be relieved by pressure on the affected artery, usually the common carotid artery or occasionally the eyeball on the affected side. When the pressure is released, there is usually a reoccurrence and resurgence of the pain.

The duration of the attack varies from individual to individual. It may be from a few minutes to several weeks. It is rarely less than three hours and is commonly eight to twenty-four hours duration. The affected artery or arteries may be very sensitive to the touch, as sometimes on the surrounding skin. Sometimes a hematoma may form around the affected vessel.

Likewise, the intensity of the attack may be variable. The intensity may vary from barely perceptible to fierce intensity. It may be influenced by walking, by bodily efforts, or sudden change in position. Sometimes it is reversed by bright light, loud sounds, and mental efforts. Intensity is often increased by lying down and reduced by sitting upright. Long exacerbations and remissions may occur, particularly in pre-menstrual migraine.

PRE-HEADACHE PHENOMENA

The pre-headache phenomena of migraine occur in about ten per cent of the people who have migraine. They are commonly post ictal such as hemianopsia and variable hallucinations of light and color. Feelings of tension and hunger and insomnia, often followed by profound sleep, may precede the headache. Some complain of decreased energy and drive, while others tell of buoyancy and talkativeness, paresthesias of the face and hands. Vertigo, beginning with a violent spinning sensation accompanied by vomiting, sweating, prostration, and agnosia, precedes some migraines, followed by intense headache and further nausea and vomiting.

Sacks talks about migraine "auras." Auras have been described as preliminary sensations of various diseases, particularly epilepsy. Migraine auras include not only the hallucinations described above, but also various kinds of affective states, various disturbances of speech and mood disorders. There are various kinds, primarily visual disturbances. The pre-migraine visual disturbances may be blind spots arranged in visual quadrants or perhaps in isolated areas of bluishness. There may be homonomous quadrants and hemionopsic field defects. These defects are usually contralateral to the side of headaches.

At times such visual disturbances may take the form of geometric designs, flashes of light, golden balls, stars, or serrations; most of these are mobile and interfere with vision. These should not be confused with the visual problems accompanying the migraine. Other kinds of auras are parasthesias of the face, hand, and foot on the contra-lateral side of the headache.

The mood disorders that precede some migraine are interesting. The patient is often seriously depressed. He is quite unsocial, irritable, and irascible, cannot make decisions and rejects responsibility. He is impulsive, hostile, and quite destructive, often directing his hostility at people who are dependent upon him. Sometimes edema will precede the headache.

It might be pertinent here to elicit some of the other kinds of aural hallucinations. Auditory hallucinations take the form of hissing, growling, sometimes a rumbling noise. Smell hallucinations are not uncommon, taking the form of intense, unpleasant smells. Visceral and epigastric symptoms are common; the most is the intense nausea, which is much more intense and quite different from that during the migraine headache. Motion hallucinations have been somewhat mentioned previously. Intense and sudden vertigo, accompanied by staggering, and sometimes, vomiting, is quite common.

The aura of Migrainous Syncope are quite interesting. They are not similar to the epileptic seizures (e.g., *petit mal*) inasmuch as here the patient goes into the syncope state in stages, i.e., it will take a few minutes before the syncope takes place and it is gradual; afterwards the patient regains his faculties in the same gradual fashion.

Some experts on the subject claim they have witnessed a convulsion during the migraine aura, but these are relatively rare. This raises an interesting question of the relation between migraine and epilepsy. Some have claimed they have seen convulsions at the height of the migraine attack. Aretaeus in the second century described such a migraine attack followed by a loss of consciousness and convulsions. Lennox calls such attacked "hybrid" seizures. I will refer to this later on in my comparison of the work I have done with idiopathic epileptics and migraine patients.

Sacks summarized the following features of the "affective states" of migraine:

1. Their sudden onset.
2. Their apparent sourcelessness, and frequent incongruity with the foreground contents of consciousness.
3. Their overwhelming quality.
4. A sense of passivity, and of the affect being "forced" into the mind.
5. Their brief duration (they rarely last more than a few minutes).
6. The sense of stillness and timelessness they convey: such states may wax in depth or intensity, but this occurs despite the absence of any experiential "happening."
7. Their difficulty or impossibility of adequate description. Such states of overwhelming "forced" feeling may occur not only in cerebral paroxysms as migraine and epilepsy, but in schizophrenic and drug-induced psychoses, in feverish and toxic states, in hysterical, ecstatic and dream-states. We are inevitably reminded of William James' listing of the qualities of "mystical" states: ineffability, noetic quality, transiency, passivity.

Sacks also believes that migraine disorders are caused by alterations in higher integrative functions, but may escape notice because of their weirdness, strangeness, and subtlety. For example, may patients claim that before and during the migraine attack that they feel "strange" or confused and will not drive home during this feeling. After these phenomena, there are the more elaborate sequences such as scintillating scotomata, bizarre alterations of perception, and illusory and dream-like states, followed by complex difficulties in perception and use of the body language, and speech disorders, and sometimes, delirious states.

INCIDENCE OF AURA OCCURRENCE, AND PREDISPOSITION

Because of the variability of the auras in migraine, it is very difficult to assess the incidence of auras, but it is estimated that about 20% of migraine patients have auras of one kind or another.

COMPARISON OF MIGRAINE AURAS AND THOSE OF EPILEPSY

Reference has already been made to the relation of epileptic seizures and migraine attacks (not auras). Hughlings Jackson writes:

> While scientifically migraine is, I think to be classified with epilepsies . . . it would be as absurd to classify it along with ordinary cases of epilepsy as to class whales with other mammals for purposes of practical life. A whale is in law a fish; in zoology it is a mammal.

There are similarities and differences in the auras of both diseases. In some migraine auras the patient will lose consciousness. Visual symptoms are far more common in migraine auras, and assume specific forms. Parasthesias occur in about twice as many migraine auras as epileptic. The rate of passage of the parasthesia auras are much faster than that of migraine. Convulsions are rare in migraine but occur more periodically in epilepsy; post ictal weakness is common in epilepsy, but rare in migraine. Alterations in higher integrative functions are about the same in both diseases, but take a different form. For example, the dissociated states of temporal lobe epileptic seizures are much more intense in epilepsy than migraine, but it is rare that few epileptics do experience the delirium which sometimes follow migraine auras. Both Gowers and Lennox have outlined the "twilight region" and in some cases there are alternating symptoms in the same patient. Liveing talks about the transformation of one paroxysm to the other. I will show later the psychological similarities of each disease.

The concept of classical migraine involving the basilar territory (so-called basilar migraine) was clearly brought to focus in 1961 by Bickerstaff. The syndrome included bilateral loss or disturbance of vision as its most important characteristic accompanied by other signs—including ataxia, dysarthvia, vertigo, tinnitus or bilateral sensory changes. An occipital pounding headache follows. Recently, it has become increasingly clear that electroencephalographic abnormalities in migraine are common, especially in children. Migraine constitutes a major cause of unexpected potentially epileptogenic abnormalities encountered in pediatric encephalography and when such unexpected EEG discharges are found, a history of migraine can often be elicited.

Camfield et al describe four patients having classical migraine which because of total visual loss, strongly suggests involvement of the basilar artery. All have had seizures which can be easily controlled and all had remained normal with a "good" personality, despite their angry and very active EEG abnormalities. The authors believe that here a causal relationship between migraine and seizure abnormalities exists. In three cases, the epileptic manifestations to be directly triggered by the migrainous aura. In the second patient, migraine and seizures occurred separately in time. A family history of migraine was found in four cases offering further support for such a diagnosis. The authors believe that diphenylhydantoin is often beneficial in controlling and preventing common or "classical" migraine, particularly in children or adolescents. "Classical" migraine for children or adolescents is frequently a more dramatic event, both clinically and electroencephalographically than in adults. The occurrence of seizures is association in younger age groups also appears to be more common and may relate to the lower epileptic thresholds in young brains. Patients with "classical" but not clearly basilar migraine may have focal epileptic manifestations with other cerebral localization. It is likely that severe epileptiform EEG abnormalities in these children result from ischemic changes caused by repeated migraine auras in the region of the basilar artery. Although these epileptic abnormalities are electrically autonomous, they require a precipitating stimulus of a migraine aura in order to produce a clinical seizure.

Lawall and Doman report a case of a young woman taken to the emergency room diagnosed as a hysterical conversion reaction and later diagnosed by a neurologist as a basilar migraine headache.

There is another variant of migraine, which may be related to epilepsy, called acute confusional migraine (ACM), which was first described by Gascon and Barlow in four children, aged 8–16, in states of confused agitation and resembling toxic metabolic psychosis. Only one confusional episode occurred in each child, but at other times the children had typical migraine symptoms. Electroencephalographic tracings 12–24 hours subsequent to the attack demonstrated a generalized disorganization of the background with focal slowing in either the right or left posterior quadrant.

Acute confusional migraine occurs in either sex between the ages of 5–16. The acute confusional state was an initial manifestation of migraine in patients. The family history of migraine is an important clue for these patients. Confusion and disorientation are accompanied by agitation that is the mixture of apprehension and combativeness. The duration of the attack is several hours but it may vary from 10 minutes to 20 hours. Initially it was though that the confusional state was secondary to focal edema affecting the reticular activity system. It is now thought to be a vasoconstriction in the entire cortical system or a hemispheric ischemia rather than an edema of the brain stem.

It is not clear why ACM is more often encountered in children than adults. Some degree of confusion has been reported in adults with migraine but it appears to lack the element of agitation. No specific therapy has been promulgated for ACM.

PREDISPOSITION TOWARD MIGRAINE

It is held that epilepsy has a strong tendency to run in families. Lennox in studying a large population with migraine noted that 61% described a parent as having been affected with migraine (as compared with approximately 28% in our study). Friedman states that 65% of sufferers who visited a headache clinic give a family history of migraine (as compared with approximately 47% in our study). Goodell, Lewontin, and Wolff studies 119 patients with severe headache and asked about the incidence of migraine in other members of the family. In 29%, neither parent had migraine (as compared with 54% in our study); 44% with one migrainous parent had migraine (as compared with 28% in our study) and 69% with both parents affected had migraine (no data in our study). Sacks believes that, in addition to the purely genetic data, we must take into account family *environment* which may produce migraine and the only way to really compare the incidence of migraine is in identical twins separated at birth.

MIGRAINE AND OTHER PSYCHOSOMATIC DISORDERS

The incidence of other psychosomatic disorders and migraine vary from investigator to investigator. Wolff found that migraine sufferers also suffered from functional heart disease, essential hypertension, vasomotor rhinitis, certain types of respiratory infections, hay fever and asthma, ulcers, and psychoneuroses. Graham in tabulating the sicknesses of 46 migraine patients, found that one-third suffered from allergic diseases; their family history indicated that 10% (in the family) had epilepsy, 30% allergies, 29% arthritis, 60% hypertension, and 40% cerebrovascular accidents. On the other hand, Critchley has an almost opposite view:

> ... in early childhood, a migrainous constitution may manifest itself in the form of infantile eczema; a little later as travel sickness. At a slightly older age it can show itself as recurrent spells of vomiting ... Are migraine victims more or less likely to develop peptic ulcers, coronary disease, rheumatoid arthritis, or colitis? My clinical impression ... is that there exists a sort of negative correlation. Lifelong migraine seems to confer a sort of protection against the subsequent development of other stress disorders.

AGE AND MIGRAINE

Most of the literature on the age of inception of migraine states that migraine takes place relatively late in life (after the third decade).

INTERVAL BETWEEN ATTACKS

The length of time between successive attacks of migraine is somewhere between two and ten weeks. Some investigators believe that "immunity" builds up between attacks. This immunity diminishes by degrees and the likelihood of an attack increases as the immunity diminishes. As the immunity diminishes, less potent stimuli can cause an attack. When the attack does come, it can come with violent explosiveness.

PHYSIOLOGY OF MIGRAINE

Some medical people think that migraine is an allergic reaction, but this has never been proven. Wolff has studied the physiology of migraine rather extensively and has shown fairly conclusively that the intensity of migraine is proportional to the dilation of the extra cranial arteries and could be mitigated by manual compression or adrenaline on the dilated artery. He has postulated the theory of cortical ischemia as the etiology of the scotomata. Sacks, on the other hand, discounts this theory as too simplistic and unproven.

The chemical theories of migraine revolve around three—that of histamine, acetylcholine and 5-Hydroxytryptamine acting at the synaptic junctions of the parasympathetic nervous system. The first two do not hold much water. However, in 1961 it was observed that migrainous attacks could be induced by taking senipasil, and the attacks could be dispersed by the intravenous infusion of 5-Hydroxytryptamine.

Nattero et al studied 18 patients suffering from menstrual migraine and 11 control subjects. The platelet sensitivity to prostacyclin (PS) and the platelet content of 5 PHT was assessed. Also investigated both in the basal condition (follicular phase of the cycle) and during the migraine attack the levels of anxiety and depression were assessed. The trends observed in the two groups are significantly different for both PS (p, .02) and 5-PHT ($p < .01$). This suggests the hypothesis that a change in the platelet hypothesis evident in the luteal cycle and premenstrual phase of the cycle, can play a remarkable role in menstrual migraine pathogenesis. From the psychological point of view the patients are normal even if they are significantly less introverted, more anxious and depressed than controls.

Insofar as EEG findings in migraine, despite the large number of studies with EEGs on migraine patients, there is no specific pattern as there is with epileptic patients (i.e., the wave and spike patterns).

EXPERIMENTAL DESIGN

One hundred and seven migraine patients, 15 males and 92 females, were given a questionnaire designed essentially to assess various psychological aspects of the patient's disease. In addition to identifying data such as age, sex, diagnosis, medication, marital status, date symptoms first noticed, and what they were, the life change unit (LCU) self-concept was explored as kinds of psychological disturbance at time of occurrence of symptoms, i.e., stress, loss of someone close before, difficulty with career and money were assessed. Various other psychosomatic manifestations, such as enuresis, tics, were assessed during childhood and adulthood. Subjective estimates of psychological variables, such as ambition, persistence, dependency, expressions of grief and rage, conformity, were obtained. Frequency and type of nocturnal dreams were also assessed. Familial information, such as personality of parents, which parent was dominant in the home, and incidence of psychosomatic disturbance, were also obtained, including how well patient got along with employer, employees, and other persons. Strength of religious beliefs was obtained for each patient. Finally, the influence of external stimuli on each patient was assessed.

The questionnaire was analyzed for the group of migraine patients for each question.

In addition, each patient was given the Multiple-Affect Checklist, the Holtzman Ink Blot Test, and the Cornell Index, the latter a test of psychosomatic illness.

RESULTS

Most of the patients in this study were married. Divorced and widowed constituted a goodly percentage of this group. By far the greatest percentage of familial members who experience headaches were mothers of these patients. Various kinds of difficulties just previous to the onset of the migraine headaches had little or nothing to do with their onset. All patients thought they were seriously or moderately disabled previous to their headaches. Reaction of friends, relatives, and acquaintances were rather consistent. Forty-six percent of the relatives were either greatly or moderately upset by their (the patients') migraines, while 50% of the friends were greatly, moderately, or mildly upset, while only approximately 20% of the acquaintances were mildly, moderately, or greatly upset. Only a relatively small percent (27%) lost anyone by death, moving, etc., close to them before onset of symptoms. About one-fourth of these patients had migraine headaches often as children, so that early onset of such headaches was to some extent a precursor of migraine as adults. Tremors, tics, and convulsions, and enuresis, stuttering, and heart pains as a child did not seem hardly, if at all, evident in these patients; but temper tantrums do, again to some extent, seem to be a percursor of migraine in these patients, since 23% did have temper tantrums as a child. The biting of nails also seems to be fairly prominent in the childhood behavior of these patients since 23% bit their nails quite often as children. Twenty-one percent are having tremors as adults (7.7% quite often; 3.8% very often; 11.5% moderately often). Likewise a moderate amount has tics (19%) as an adult. The temper tantrums as children (23%) seemed to have somewhat mitigated as adults (7%), although somewhat less so in the case of biting nails (23% as children, 19% as adults). Relatively few of any of these patients had convulsions, enuresis, stuttered, had heart pains, or sucked their thumbs as adults. However, 27% said they got angry easily, and tangential to this, 42% said they were moody. Ambition, cleanliness, persistence, and *good control* seemed to be part of the dynamics of a goodly number of these migraine patients. Strangely enough almost 86% said they were able to express grief (as compared to 27% who said they got angry easily and 42% who said they were able to express rage). Ninety-six percent were able to express joy, while 76% said they could express other emotions. Evidently this was a conforming group. Most of these patients (73%) conformed to everyday mores.

Dreaming and dream life were an interesting aspect of the behavior of these patients. Well over half of this sample dreamed either once every few nights or practically every night, and 85% said their dreams were either very or moderately clear. Unfortunately we did not assess what these migraine patients dreamed about. A majority of these patients said they daydreamed and about half said they daydreamed everyday or once every few days. Over 50% said their daydreams were very clear or moderately clear. In a majority of the cases, the mother was the disciplinarian when the patient was growing up. Relatively few of these patients' relatives had psychosomatic ailments. Insofar as work is concerned, these patients seemed to have done very well on the job. The majority enjoyed the work on their last job, got (or getting) along with bosses, and got along with their fellow employees.

It is rather interesting and somewhat significant that approximately the same percentage (19.2) had their symptoms increase under certain weather conditions and at certain seasons. A much larger percentage said that certain external stimuli induced their headaches. For example, 31% said that artificial light induced their headaches, 23% said noise induced their migraine, 27% said temperature changes induced their headaches, and a surprising 58% said tactile sensations induced their headaches.

What can we gather from the mass of empirical and speculative data on migraine? From this study, there seems to be a familial diathesis or the tendency for it to occur on the mother's side. It is quite a disturbing affliction to the patient but somewhat less disturbing to relatives and friends. Most migraine develops as adults. The migraine patients here got angry easily and were unable to express rage. Ambition, cleanliness, persistence, and nonconformance are characteristic of the migraine patients. As in many psychosomatic ailments, when the patient becomes emotionally upset the migraine becomes worse.

Probably the most startling result of the questionnaire of these patients was the fact that external stimuli such as light, heat, and sound precipitated migraine headaches. Here we have an etiology similar to that of idiopathic epilepsy, that is, in some instances a migraine headache can be triggered by such stimuli, as well as epileptic convulsions. Future research may tell what kind of stimulus will trigger what kind of migraine, how long it will take for the migraine to take effect, and how long it will last, as well as the intensity of the headache.

The test results indicate that these migraine patients were a depressed group who were confused, in conflict and convalescent themselves, maladjusted and neurotic. They had an obsessive compulsive diathesis, were generally immature, and according to the Holtzman could not tolerate stress.

Another point which is of interest to both physicians and patients is that all patients in this sample were being treated by physicians. Phillips believes that headache sufferers who go to physicians are in general more neurotic and suffer more pain than those who do not consult physicians. So far as is known to this author (Geist) there are no studies which differentiate the psychodynamics of migraine patients who go to physicians and those that do not go to physicians. There is the possibility that the group in this project were more affluent, had more persistent symptomatology, and believed in the efficacy of physicians, since they did have a goodly amount of psychopathology.

CHAPTER 3

The question of comparability of any set of diseases is complicated by the sets of measures used for comparison. Ideally in psychosomatic medicine it should be both in the physiological (organic) and psychological/psychiatric realm. However, so far as is known to this author there are few if any comparisons (or contrasts) in the purely medical area, although there have been investigations into isolated conditions. Since in the preceding conditions which I have studied, I have primarily pursued the emotional area, comparability will be adhered to primarily in this area, and deductions made from the results and inferences made to all psychosomatic diseases. Since initial evidence was made from questionnaires, perhaps this would be a good starting point.

Questionnaires were administered in three conditions: rheumatoid arthritis, cardiac, and migraine patients. The "core" of the questionnaires in each were the same with some modifications for each of the conditions.*

In all these diseases, the conditions may be termed "chronic," since the average time the rheumatoid patients had their disease was 10 years and almost all the heart patients had their conditions over 2 years. Relatively few if any of the conditions lost some one close, had difficulty with career or money or had mental stress just previous to their illness. All perceived their ailment as moderately or severely disabling. The analysis of other psychosomatic conditions is rather interesting. It does not appear that any of the psychosomatic conditions assessed as an adult or child in any of these illnesses were present to any extent, if at all. Thus, in these psychosomatic diseases (heart disease, rheumatoid arthritis, migraine) previous to the ailment, psychosomatic conditions were not present, with the possible exception of migraine patients, where there was a mild tendency to have temper tantrums (23%), tremors (23%) and biting of nails (23% as children, 19% as adults). In the rheumatoid arthritis group, there seems to be a definite familial diathesis, in the arteriosclerotic group there was a definite familial diathesis while the valvular and disturbance of conduction group had a possible familial diathesis. In the migraine group there was a definite familial diathesis on the mother's side. Here we see a commonality which is clear and precise. In all these conditions, the disease occurred in some member of the family and in some cases more than one.

Insofar as anger is concerned, anger seemed to be a precipitating agent in the hypertensives (60%) and the rheumatoids (60%) but only 27% of the

---

*See pp. ••–•• appendix for questionnaire in each.

migraine patients said they got angry easily but tangential to this 42% said they were moody. In the rheumatoids and all the heart patients, they got along well with other members of the family (primarily parents and siblings); there is no data on this with the migraine patients). Disciplinarian in the family in the rheumatoids was primarily the mother, the mother in the arteriosclerotics, the father in the hypertensives, split evenly with the mother and father in the valvular and disturbance of conduction group.

Insofar as ability to express rage is concerned, the primary emotion, rage, with which we are concerned here, 75% of the rheumatoids were unable to express rage, while the only heart group clearly unable to express rage were the disturbance of conduction group; 52% of the migraine group were unable to express rage. It is rather interesting that all the rheumatoids and cardiac patients considered themselves extremely clean and neat, and a majority of the migraines thought they were neat and clean. The majority of heart patients and migraine patients perceived themselves as ambitious, but there is no data on the rheumatoids on this variable. Insofar as dreams are concerned, dreams were not frequent in the rheumatoids or heart groups but were frequent in the migraine group. All three groups had dreams which were clear or moderately clear. (Because of time commitments I was not able to delineate what any of the three groups dreamed about). Exercise and inclement weather seem to be either a precipitating agent or made symptoms worse with the rheumatoids while emotional upset increased symptoms with the hypertensives, valvular, and disturbance of conduction patients; exercise increased symptoms with the majority of arteriosclerotic and valvular, and weather and seasons had no influence whatsoever in the heart patients. With the migraines, a small percentage (19%) had symptoms increase under certain weather conditions and at certain seasons but significantly (as opposed to rheumatoid and heart patients) migraine patients had their symptoms triggered by artificial light, noise, temperature change and tactile sensations. Diet had no influence whatsoever with the rheumatoids, but fatty foods did have an influence on all heart patients, and certain foods such as chocolate, Chinese foods, red wine and certain cheeses may be precipitating agents in migraine headache.

It is rather interesting that insofar as etiology is concerned, that there are only three commonality factors—chronicity, familial diathesis, and diet as precipitating agent (although with each condition, different kinds of foods precipitate different conditions). Insofar as behavioral aspects are concerned, there are numerous aspects of commonality. All perceived their ailment as disabling and surprisingly enough, none had either a psychosomatic condition as a child or stress or difficulty with career or money just previous to their ailment; all got along well with other members of their family and all had good work situations previous to their condition. All were ambitious and considered themselves clean and neat. Finally, in all the conditions, the mother was the disciplinarian.

There were also some other surprising results. Except for the hypertensives, anger was not a precipitating agent in any of the conditions. Dreams were not frequent except in the migraines. Three other results, not surprising, were that except in the hypertensives exercise was a precipitating agent, and except for migraines, light, noise, temperature change and tactile sensations were not a precipitating agent and except for rheumatoids, inclement weather was not a precipitating agent. To put it another way, in the hypertensives only, anger was a precipitating agent, in the migraines only, light, noise, temperature change and tactile sensations were a precipitating agent and in the rheumatoids only, inclement weather was a precipitating agent.

TEST RESULTS

The test results are embellished by the fact that a number of conditions were tested but by the same token essentially different tests were used for different conditions. Perhaps a compromise can be made for the same tests for the same conditions.

Insofar as total number of symptoms across the board in all diseases, bizarre ideation seems to be the most frequent, with depression and hostility next, followed by narcisstic impulses and a rich inner life and aggression, anxiety and sexual abnormality. Obsessive compulsive traits and low ego strength were also part of the symptomology. The condition which had the most number of pathological responses was epilepsy followed by rheumatoid arthritis, heart disease (all kinds), migraine, atopic dermatitis, acne and hand eczema. Insofar as symptoms are concerned, the conditions which had the greatest spread (spread in terms of most number of psychopathological elements) were bizarre ideation, (8), aggression, anxiety and depression (5), hostility, obsessive compulsive impulses and narcissism (4) and conflict, and sexual difficulties (3). Lack of ego strength, regression and depression did not seem to have much influence in these conditions.

COMMENTS

Evidently in the diseases studied here, bizarre ideation is a constant and pervasive element in their psychopathology. One wonders whether

TABLE II
SUMMARY OF QUESTIONS IN QUESTIONNAIRE FOR VARIOUS CONDITIONS

	Rheumatoids		Heart						Disturbance of Conduction		Migraine	
			Arteriscrerotics		Hypertensive		Valvular					
	Yes	No	Yes	No	Yes	No	Yes	No	Yes	No	Yes	No
1. Chronic (over 2 years)	X		X		X		X		X		X	
2. Difficulty with career or money or stress previous to condition		X		X		X		X		X		X
3. Perception of ailment as severely or moderately disabling	X		X		X		X		X		X	
4. Presence of other psychosomatic conditions as child		X		X		X		X		X		X
5. Familial Diathesis	X		X			X	X		X		X	
6. Anger as precipitating agent	X			X	X			X		X		X
7. Repression of anger	X			X		X		X	X			X
8. Got along well with other members of family	X		X		X		X		X			
9. Mother disciplinarian	X		X		X		X		X			
10. Father disciplinarian					X							
11. Considered selves clean and neat	X		X		X		X		X		X	
12. Ambitious	X		X		X		X		X		X	
13. Frequent dreams		X		X		X		X		X	X	
14. Precipitating agents												
A. Exercise	X		X			X	X		X			
B. Foods	X		X		X		X			X	X	
C. Inclement weather	X			X		X		X		X		X
15. Light, noise, temperature change, tactile		X		X		X		X		X	X	
16. Work situation before onset good	X		X		X		X		X		X	

TABLE III

Elements in Common With All Patients	*Elements in Common Except One Condition*	*Exception*
1. Chronicity	1. Anger not precipitating agent	1. Hypertensives
2. Perception of ailment as severely or moderately disabling	2. Infrequent dreams	2. Migraine
3. Familial Diatheses	3. Exercise precipitating agent	3. Hypertensives
4. Work situation good	4. Light, noise, temperature change tactile sensations did not precipitate condition	4. Migraine
5. Got along well with other members of family	5. Inclement weather not precipitating agent	5. Rheumatoids
6. Consider self clean and neat		
7. Diet as precipitating agent (varies with various conditions)		
8. Good work situation		
9. No difficulty with career or money		
10. Absence of psychosomatic conditions		
11. Mother disciplinarian		
12. Ambitious		

TABLE IV
TABULATION OF SYMPTOMATOLOGY BY DISEASE

	According to Testing							
	Aggression	*Anxiety*	*Hostility*	*Narcissistic or Introspective*	*Lack Ego Strength*	*Conflict*	*Depression*	*Repression*
Epilepsy	2	1	2	1	1	2	2	1
Rheumatoid arthritis	1	1	1	2	1	0	1	0
Heart disease (total)	0	1	3	1	0	0	0	0
Dermatoses								
A. Acne	0	0	0	0	0	0	1	0
B. Atopic Dermatitis	2	1	0	0	0	0	0	0
C. Psoriasis	0	1	0	2	0	1	2	0
D. Eczema of Hand	0	0	1	0	0	0	0	0
Migraine	0	0	0	0	0	1	1	0
	5	5	7	6	2	4	7	1

TABLE IV—Continued
TABULATION OF SYMPTOMATOLOGY BY DISEASE

According to Testing						*Miscellaneous*			
Self Comp.	*Repression*	*Homosexuality*	*Sexual Difficulties*	*Bizarre Ideation*	*Cannot Tolerate Stress*	*Burnt Child*	*Strong Bond With Mother*	*Psycho-logical Impotency*	*Defensive Wall*
0	1	1	1	1	0	1	1	0	0
1	0	0	0	2	0	0	0	0	0
0	0	0	0	1	0	0	0	0	1
1	0	0	0	2	0	0	0	0	0
1	0	0	1	2	0	0	0	0	0
1	0	0	0	1	0	0	0	0	0
0	0	0	1	1	0	0	0	1	0
0	0	0	0	7	1	0	0	0	0
4	1	1	3	17	1	1	1	1	1

TABLE V
TOTAL NUMBER OF PSYCHOPATHOLOGICAL TRAITS FROM TESTING IN ALL PSYCHOSOMATIC CONDITIONS

Trait	*Number*	
1. Bizarre ideation	13	(including schizophrenic trends)
2. Hostility	7	
3. Depression	7	
4. Narcissism	7	
5. Aggression	5	
6. Anxiety	5	
7. Sexual Repression	5	
8. Conflict	4	
9. Obsessive compulsive	4	
10. Low ego strength	2	
11. Regression	1	
12. Homosexuality	1	
13. Cannot tolerate stress	1	
14. Burnt child constellation	1	
15. Psychological impotency	1	

there is in psychosomatic conditions an element of psychosis or at the least neurosis. Aggression, anxiety, depression and hostility also seem to be potent forces in their dynamics.

Thus, in addition to the various psychopathological symptoms listed above, familial diathesis and diet also seem to be etiological factors in these diseases. Stress has been found to be a common factor in all diseases (not only psychosomatic), but surprisingly this was not the case in these instances. While the above psychopathology certainly has implications for stress, stress itself was not mentioned by the patients either in the questionnaire or rarely in the test results as an etiological factor. There are some indigenous factors specific to certain disease, for example anger for hypertensives, exercise for all disease except hypertensives and light, temperature change, noise and tactile sensations for migraine and inclement weather for rheumatoids.

Thus, we can say that familial diathesis, diet and possibly exercise, are precipitating agents and bizarre ideation, aggression, anxiety, depression, hostility and overwhelming ambition were common personality characteristics. With these as starting agents, let us examine the implications and relevancy to the other psychosomatic illnesses.

It might be worth while here first to see if we can get an explanation summary of the results of both the questionnaires and testing for the various conditions studied. An inspection of "the elements in common with all patients" on the questionnaire, certain of these elements stand out to the author as being important. These are *chronicity, familial diathesis,* and *diet* as precipitating agents. An inspection of "elements in common except one condition" (disease), certain elements appear to be important; these are: anger *not* a precipitating agent, and *exercise* a precipitating agent (except hypertensives). An inspection of "elements in common except two conditions," we see that *repression* of anger (exceptions are migraine and valvular heart condition), is the only precipitating agent. Evidently in the psychosomatic conditions studied here, all the diseases were chronic, all had a tendency for the disease to run in the family, and diet had something to do with the onset of their condition (not necessarily the same diet). It is interesting that "stress" is far down on the list of elements as a precipitating agent, which most investigators believe is the primary cause of psychosomatic conditions. A surprising finding is that exercise is a precipitating agent in all conditions (except hypertensives). This is especially surprising in a condition such as migraine. It also seems that repressed anger is a precipitating agent in some conditions and not in others.

Insofar as testing is concerned, running down the list, we see that bizarre ideation is by far the most numerous psychopathological syndrome in this group with depression and hostility also important agents. Narcissistic impulses also seem to be important, are aggression, anxiety, and sexual abnormalities, obsessive compulsive tendencies and low ego strength seem to be moderate agents with various other syndromes such as homosexuality, not being able to tolerate stress, repression, impotence, and a "burnt child constellation" being far down the list, and having slight influence on the etiology of the psychosomatic conditions studied here.

It might be useful here to compare the results obtained with those of other investigations in the whole field of psychosomatic medicine. Nemiah and Sifneos describe all psychosomatic patients as "alexithymic;" they are incapable of perceiving and verbalizing their fantasy bound moods and are governed by their uncontrolled emotions, e.g. by impulsively surfacing, mostly negative affects such as anger and irritation. They are unable to let conflicts emerge so that they can be worked out in fantasy or imagination.

There is a "school" of psychosomatic medicine known as the "Parisian School" who regard psychosomatic patients as having "regressive ego" which intensifies with their dealing with other people. This manifests itself in that the psychosomatic patient cannot distinguish between him (her) self and other people, "The relationship between closeness and psychic distance cannot be mastered," and such patients cannot relate and show absolute emptiness in their relationship with others. The other person does not exist with a value of his (her) own (what they call "relation blanche"). Other people are exchangeable, and possess only instrumental value for the patient ("comportament operatoire"). They have a "weak libidinal valence" of their own self system and other person's diminished significance in it. Thus no one can play a decisive role, not even the therapist. Of course, not only psychosomatic patients show these characteristics, but also many others (narcissistic, schizophrenic, etc.) but according to the Parisian School, this is particularly characteristic of psychosomatics.

Undoubtedly there is a relationship between this author's findings and those of the above groups. In consonance with the Parisian School, narcissistic characteristics are important in my group and bizarre ideation and conflict in consonance with the Nemiah and Sifneos findings.

PAIN

Pain is a common syndrome in many diseases and many psychosomatic conditions although not universally so. In the conditions that this author studied, pain was a syndrome in the rheumatoid arthritis and myocardial infarction patients. In others e.g. epileptic, dermatoses, hypertensives, disturbances of conduction, and valvular, pain was occasional and peripheral.

Lambert studied the coping mechanism in rheumatoid arthritis. Coping with the existing pain, disabling effects and/or defenses brought about by rheumatoid arthritis is not an easy task for the afflicted person. To cope with the physical aspects of the disease, the afflicted person is likely to use the coping mechanisms of information seeking, direct action, inhibition of action, intra-psychic processes and social support.

Skevington reviewed pain in rheumatoid arthritis from a socio-cognitive perspective. Questions are raised about the usefulness of the distinction between organic and non organic patients and alternative explanations are given for sero negative patients. A case based on physiology and behavior is made for more studies of acute and prechronic stages of rheumatoid arthritis. Four major areas of methodology are considered:

1. Studies of explanations about rheumatoid arthritis show that people hold relatively accurate views about the nature of pain in rheumatoid arthritis and where causal explanation are given for pain and illness this is conducive to good mental health.
2. A section on the measurement of pain addresses issues about the applicability and the standardization of scales and welcomes the move from exclusive to qualitative multidimensional measures. The pain language of rheumatoid arthritis is described.
3. Experimental studies of pain in rheumatoid arthritis appear to be of limited use.
4. A review of activities and functional disabilities indicate that cognitive and behavior modification techniques appear to have the most premise in motivating chronic patients to be more active and to comply with medication as much as improving mental health. In a discussion of successful therapies the principle of reducing uncertainty and increasing perception of control are the underlying features.

Ramsay believes that certain personality dynamics are exhibited by all pain patients. There are hysterical conversion (including globus hystericus, fainting, either neurotic hyperventilation of psychotic, sometimes agitated); hypochrondical and obsessional states (those obsessed with the idea of pain). Hypochondriacal patients with pain are usually the paranoid type.

In the patients studied in my group, although hysterical conversion symptoms were not a cardinal syndrome, depression, hypochondriacal and obsessive compulsive states were moderate symptomatic states.

EPILEPSY

Although in previous chapters, I have made comparisons (and contrasts) of my findings with those of others in specific psychosomatic conditions, it might be useful to delineate this again.

Some of the more modern writers on epilepsy, such as Pincus and Tucker, believe that psychopathology in the epileptic is more frequent in psychomotor epilepsy while Barker considers the epileptic "spell" due to maladaptation of the environment. This is not quite the same as I found in my research.

Cobb has made some interesting personality discoveries concerning rheumatoid arthritis. He found that rheumatoid arthritics perceive their mother as being mean and a source of undeserved punishment; they perceive their parents more often as being strict with discipline; women with rheumatoid arthritis are more likely to come from high status stress families. The MMPI profiles for rheumatoid arthritis patients have been reported as being statistically higher than those of controls with regard to the scales for hypochondriacs, depression, and hysteria. Moldofsky and Chester have delineated two mood patterns in rheumatoid arthritis patients. These are described as "synchronous" in which anxiety or hostility closely preceded or accompanied increases in joint tenderness and "feeling of helplessness" paradoxical in which there was an inverse relationship between the intensity of joint tenderness and feeling of helplessness. Two years after the initial observation, the patients in the "paradoxical" group were far less well than the ones in the synchronous group. Ross claims that rheumatoid arthritis patients have a depressive neurosis and have another medical illness in which emotional factors play a part, e.g. a duodenal ulcer. Personal conflicts have been of long standing and the beginning of an exacerbation will found to have occurred within a few weeks of some change in life circumstances. These patients do not readily express anger and yet are sensitive to being slighted and concerned about rivalry with others for attention. Russell compared anxiety neurotics and arthritics. Anxiety neurotics live more in a world full of frightening possibilities, are isolated and dependent, and are able to relate their symptoms in minute detail while arthritics see their future as ordered and understandable.

There is some similarity between the findings of the personality dynamics and my patients and some of the above investigators. Repressed anger was one of the cardinal characteristics of my research and the MMPI highest scores were Hs, Sc and Hy as compared Hs, D and Hy found by Cobb. My findings also paralleled somewhat those of Moldofsky and Chester.

DERMATOSES

Laihiner offers a classification of psychocutaneous disease and examines factors which result in itching and scratching becoming chronic. Pruritis is a very common sensation in dermatoses. All forms of itching whatever the cause may be intensified under emotional stress. Seven diagnostic groups totalling 99 patients, dermatitis herpetiformis, lichen ruber planus, cireo m senipta, lichen corneus, obtusus and pruritus psychogenes. The findings were:

1. The different mechanisms by which skin disease becomes chronic had a psychological background.
2. Psychiatric disturbances were clearly more common than in the average population.
3. Psychosomatics is of considerable importance to explain the mechanism where the disease is not sufficiently understood.

The dermatoses in general are thought by most investigators to be due to stressful situations and unresolved and predominantly unconscious emotional conflicts. Also a disturbance in the mother-child relationship can facilitate conditioning that may lead to psychodermatoses in adolescence and maturity. Insofar as specific dermatoses are concerned, in the dermatitis urticuria, Saul believes that urticuria is a substitute for a suppressed crying, and intense longing for love may increase allergic sensitivity. In Amsterdam, Holland, a study there showed a number of interesting dynamics in urticuria.

Heavy loads of partial conscious anxiety were found to coincide with a high degree of anxiety tolerance. Violent feelings of rage and resentment were strongly averted. These patients were greatly annoyed before the urticuria attack; these patients had concealed their anger and were very distressed because of pent up anger.

Greenhill and Finesinger found that hostile feelings and depressive traits were found in patients with atopic dermatitis. My findings were the same, but I also found existence of psychological impotency, anxiety and disturbance in the sexual area.

Puca et al believe that acne excoriee is a self infected skin condition in which the sufferer has an urge to pick red, ingrained anceform lesions and which results in worsening and spreading of the acne. Although the condition is considered to be a neurotic manifestation of the patient, traditional psychiatric treatment has proven to be unsuccessful.

Cohen reviewed the beliefs of modern writers on psychogenic factors in acne. These reviews can be grouped under two headings: personality deviations in patients suffering from acne and secondly the relationship between the occurrence of acne and the sex life of its sufferers.

Egeinan suggested that the mechanism of the production of acne might be the effects of emotional stimulation and contacts with the opposite sex on hormone productivity. Sutton states that acne patients are usually depressed. Hodgson states that nervous stress, "unsettlement" and sexual difficulties can aggravate the conditions. Wittkower, Russell and Brian studied 64 acne patients and found the personality dynamics can be classified under four headings: 1. Rigid personality 2. Rebellious and fantasizing 3. Regressive (overgrown children) and 4. Sufferers from gross psychological disorders.

My own findings in acne* agree primarily with those of Wittkower and Russell. My patients had sexual difficulties, had an overproductive thought content, related poorly to their own body image, and developed conversion symptoms.

In studies by Jelliffe and Evans, on psoriasis, they found that psoriatric eruptions represent an exhibitionistic substitute which were shown to be hysterical conversion symptoms.

Wittkower and Russell studied 86 psoriasis patients and found that they were divided by clinical classification into (1) compulsive, (2) overaggressive and unaggressive (3) bisexual, (4) phobic and (5) hysterical types. The number of emotionally maladjusted in this group is far in excess of a cross section of the population or of a random sample. The authors conclude that an emotional crisis of a specific nature to the individual assumes the catalyst to mobilize a dormant predisposition.

The most recent (1990) research in psoriasis is the work of Doctor Eugene Farber and his colleagues at the Psoriasis Research Institute in Palo Alto, California. Doctor Farber was formerly Chair of the Department of Dermatology at the Stanford University Medical Center.

He suggests a psychoneuroimmunologic hypothesis. The reaction that triggers psoriatric outbursts or outbreaks can be thought of as having not only the classical causes such as burns and other trauma but also an external cause, emotional stress. Both the externally and internally induced reactions may be mediated through a common mechanism, release of potent neuropeptides by the peripheral nerve fibers of the skin thereby initiating an inflammatory waterfall that results in a psoriatic lesion in genetically predisposed individuals. Doctor Farber describes this as the new frontier in cutaneous neuroscience and presents a plausible explanation for many of the cardinal features of skin disease. Thus the neuroendocrine system is the link between emotional stress and psoriasis. Release into the circulation of stress related hormones such as ACTH by the anterior pituitary and

---

* See p. 33-34, 91-92

existence; threats of loss of an outside sense of support or disturbance to inner established patterns such as blows to self esteem or conflicts over sex and aggressiveness. A hereditary predisposition the development of eczema and respiratory disorders existed in the group studied and was particularly well marked among those who had childhood eczema; people who had childhood eczema showed a high incidence of "difficult" family positions. Eczema patients as a whole tended to have been either "unwanted" or "spoiled children" and to have been more strongly attached to one parent than the other.

My patients did not have the psychopathology characterized above. They had difficulty in the sexual area, difficulty with authority, were self conscious of their hands, and had a tendency to develop hysterical conversion symptoms—a set of psychopathology quite different from the above.

CARDIAC DISEASE

A great deal has been written about before and after the work of Friedman and Rosenman. Stevenson, Donner and Ripley found that patients with cardiac arrhythmias were anxious and insecure. They also found that hypertensive patients have grown up feeling the need to excel, but at the same time to avoid conflict or overly vigorous self assertion. These strivings often led to dilemmas and are manifested by way of tentative and non committal attitudes with respect to important interpersonal relationships and major endeavors in life. Myocardial infarction patients are typically under circumstances of emotional drain—e.g. in association with bereavement or after challenges that are unusual associated with frustration and disappointment.

The disturbance of conduction patients in my group had a much more diffuse psychopathology involving a rich inner life, little unity or integration in the self concept and a rich fantasy life. Anxiety and insecurity (compare with findings above) were only part of the package here. My hypertensive patients showed anxiety and hostility, quite different from the psychopathology described above. In contrast to only emotional drain described as part of the myocardial patients above, my patients have distinct pathological thinking and a narcissistic preoccupation with the self.

The psychosomatic symptomatology of migraine headache has been described by Wolff et al in detail above. Engle, Hamburger and Plunner maintain that migraine attacks are due to unexpressed anger and to vasospasm of branches of the internal carotid artery. Likewise, my migraine patients got angry easily and were unable to express rage. Ambition, cleanliness, persistence and non conformance are characteristic of the migraine patients and the migraine gets worse when the patient gets emotionally upset. My migraine patients were a depressed group who were confused, in conflict, maladjusted and neurotic. They had an obsessive compulsive diathesis were immature and could not tolerate stress.

The work of Moos has important implications for the environmental influences on psychosomatic diseases. He assumes that environments have unique "personalities" just as people do. Some social environments are more supportive than others. Some social environments are extremely autocratic and controlling. Some social environments strongly emphasize order, clarity and organization. Behavioral characteristics have been shown to be strong risk factors in certain diseases; environmental factors are associated with each of these high risk factors. Although this has been no secret for some time, Moos believes that the relationship of support, cohesion and involvement generally have positive effects in enhancing normal development, while system maintenance or system change dimensions such as responsibility, work pressure and change increases the likelihood of stress and disease. Moos makes an interesting point—He says "Rather than labelling the process with the global term 'stress,' it may be more fruitful to attempt to understand the specific physiological effects of distinct social, environmental dimensions. Social milieu dimensions might thus relate differentially to different physiological effects"—a more complete understanding of social environmental dimensions might enable clinicians to predict which environments would be adverse or beneficial for particular patients and to suggest specific and limited changes in environments where individuals suffer from particular symptoms. The systematic measurement of social climates could thus become an important aspect of the work of a diagnostician. This was what I was attempting to do with the results of my questionnaires in the various conditions. Let us see if this has been accomplished.

In the elements of the questionnaire in the rheumatoid arthritis study having to do with parental relationships, 90% of the rheumatoids considered their relationship with their mother as "good," 60% considered their relationship with their father as "good" and 50% said their mother and father were easy going. Thus, it seems that the familial entity of Moos, where bad relationships are considered to be psychopathological, this had very little to do with the development of psychopathology in *these* patients.

Insofar as the marital state of the cardiac patients, the marital state of these patients is an interesting phenomenon. The hypertensive patients and disturbance of conduction patients were primarily single and the arteriosclerotic primarily widowed, and the valvular separated. If it is postulated that the stresses of married life precipitates heart disease, then the family situation in the cardiac patients might be termed primarily positive. It may be that the percipitants are independent of the marital state.

APPENDICES

APPENDIX A

ARTHRITIS QUESTIONNAIRE

NAME *Age* *Address* *Telephone*

1. Date first noticed symptoms of arthritis
   a. At that time was there anything unusual happening psychologically such as:
   b. Mental stress or upset emotionally due to:
   c. Loss of someone close to you? If so, what relation?
   d. Difficulty with career or money
   e. Other
2. Do you think you are badly disabled because of your arthritis?
3. What is the reaction of your relatives, friends or associates to arthritis?
4. Have you lost anyone (by death, moving, etc.) close to you before or after symptoms?
   a. If so, what were the change in symptoms?
5. As a child did you have:
   1. Headache
   2. Tremors
   3. Tics
   4. Convulsions
   5. Enuresis (after 4 yrs. age)
   6. Temper tantrums
   7. Stuttering
   8. Heart pains
   9. Bite nails
   10. Suck thumb

   a. Do you have any of these now?
6. Do you get angry easily?
   a. Is there any kind of person that gets you angry?
7. Do exhibitionists or showoffs bother you?
8. Do you withdraw from difficult situations? If so, explain.
9. (Males) Have you ever been interested in active sports (swimming etc.) before symptoms?
   a. If so, degree of activity
10. (Females) Are you interested in cooking or other household duties?
11. Do you dream at all? Frequency Duration Vividness About What
12. Are you married? Single? Divorced?
    If divorced, alleged reason
    State heterosexual relations (sexual identification)
13. How do you feel about the doctor examining you?
    a. Are you satisfied with the treatment you are getting? If not, why not?
14. Have you strong religious beliefs?
15. Work history Current employment How long?
    Salary (optional) Enjoy current work? How getting along with boss?
    Other employees Other kind of work you would rather do

16. Do you consider yourself a clean person? Degree
17. Are you able to express your feelings adequately or do you repress them?
    a. Expression of: Grief Joy Rage Other emotions
18. Do you daydream? If so, what about?
19. What kind of a person do you think you are? (self concept)
    a. Do you think you are adequate? b. Inadequate c. Dependent
    d. Independent
20. In relation to your family, describe:
    a. Mother's personality and how you got along with her
    b. Father's personality and how you got along with him
    c. Sib's personality and how you got along with them
21. In your home when you were growing up:
    a. Who was disciplinarian?
    b. Was mother (surrogate) a good housekeeper
22. Did anyone else in family have arthritis?
    a. What is feeling or your family about arthritis?
23. Do you or did any members of your family have any psychosomatic ailments? (No organic cause) If so, who and what illness?
24. Does your arthritis bother you more:
    a. When you are emotionally upset? b. When you exercise?
    c. Under certain weather conditions? d. At certain seasons?
    e. Other times?
25. What do you think is the cause of your arthritis?
    (Any evidence that patient is using arthritis to get own way or secondary gains?)

APPENDIX B

HEART DISEASE QUESTIONNAIRE

(To be administered by Psychologist. Not to be administered by patient directly.)

____
Diagnosis

____
Medication

______________ ______________ ______________ ______
Name Address Telephone Age

______________ __ __ __ __ ______________
Marital Status M S W D Anyone else in family have heart disease?

______________ ______________
Date first notice symptoms What were they?

At That Time

a. Anything unusual happening psychologically such as:

1. Mental stress or upset emotionally due to:

a. Loss of someone close to you? ______ If so, what relation? ______
b. Difficulty with career or money? ______
c. Other? ______________

To What Extent Do You Think You Are Disabled?:

1. Severely Disabled ____ 2. Moderately Disabled ____ 3. Not Disabled ____

What is the reaction of your relatives, friends, or acquaintances to your heart trouble:

	Indifferent	Greatly Upset	Moderately Upset	Mildly Upset	Other
Relatives	______	______	______	______	______
Friends	______	______	______	______	______
Acquaintances	______	______	______	______	______

Have you lost anyone (by death, moving, etc.) close to you before or after symptoms?

______________ ______________ ______________ ______________ ______
Father Mother Other Blood Relative Other Person (Relationship) None

If so, what were the changes in the symptoms? ______________

HEART DISEASE QUESTIONNAIRE - 2

As a child or adult, did you or do you have: (Please circle appropriate number)

1. Very often (Every Day)
2. Quite Often (Once every three days)
3. Moderately Often (Between one a week and one a month)
4. Hardly ever (Once or less)
5. Never

	Child	Adult
Headaches	1 2 3 4 5	1 2 3 4 5
Tremors	1 2 3 4 5	1 2 3 4 5
Tics	1 2 3 4 5	1 2 3 4 5
Convulsions	1 2 3 4 5	1 2 3 4 5
Enuresis (Bedwetting after 4 years of age)	1 2 3 4 5	1 2 3 4 5
Temper Tantrums	1 2 3 4 5	1 2 3 4 5
Stuttering	1 2 3 4 5	1 2 3 4 5
Heart Pains	1 2 3 4 5	1 2 3 4 5
Bite Nails	1 2 3 4 5	1 2 3 4 5
Suck Thumb	1 2 3 4 5	1 2 3 4 5

Do you get angry easily? ________ Yes ________ No

Do you withdraw from difficult situations? ________ Yes ________ No

If so, explain: ____

Comments ____

Do you consider yourself:

	Yes	No
1. An ambitious person	___	___
2. A persistent person	___	___
3. Have good control of yourself	___	___
4. A moody person	___	___

If yes, explain when you have change in moods ____________________

	Yes	No
5. A clean person	___	___

6. A dependent independent adequate inadequate person? (circle)

7. Are you able to express your feelings adequately or do you repress them?

   Expression of: Grief ______ Able ______ Unable   Joy ______ Able ______ Unable

   Rage ______ Able ______ Unable   Other emotions ______ Able ______ Unable

8. Do you conform most of the time to everyday mores? ______ Yes ______ No

HEART DISEASE QUESTIONNAIRE - 3

9. Do you dream at all? ________

   Frequency: Practically every night ____ Once every few nights ____
   One night per week ____ Less than one night per week ____

   Vividness: Very clear ____ Moderately Clear ____ Jumbled Up ____

   Duration: All night ____ Half the night ____ Less than 1/2 night ____

10. Do you daydream? ________

    Frequency: Practically every day ____ Once every few days ____
    One day per week ____ Less than one day per week ____

    Vividness: Very Clear ____ Moderately Clear ____ Jumbled Up ____

    What about? ____

11. In relation to your family, describe:

    a. Mother's personality and how you got along with her ____________
    b. Father's personality and how you got along with him ____________
    c. Siblings' personality and how you got along with them ____________
    ____

12. In your home when you were growing up:

    a. Who was disciplinarian: ____ ____ ____________
    Father Mother Other person, relationship

13. What is the feeling in your family about heart disease? ____________

14. Do you or did any members of your family have any psychosomatic ailments, that is, sicknesses which have no apparent physical cause? ________

    If yes: ____ ____ ________________ ____
    Mother Father Other blood relative, relationship None

15. Work History: Current employment or last job ________________
    How long? ________ Dates ____________
    Enjoy current work or last job? ________ How getting along with boss or got along with boss? ___ ___ ___ Other employees ___ ___ ___
    good fair badly good fair badly

    Past work ________________ ___
    Type None

    How got along with boss ___ ___ ___ Other employees ___ ___ ___
    good fair badly good fair badly

HEART DISEASE QUESTIONNAIRE - 4

16. Have you strong religious beliefs?

    1. Extremely religious (go to place of worship regularly and observe all religious holidays) _______
    2. Moderately religious (go to place of worship occasionally and observe some holidays) _______
    3. Rarely go to place of worship _______
    4. Never go to place of worship and never observe holidays _______

17. How much did you indulge in the following previous to heart condition?

    a. Alcohol

    1. Great deal (get inebriated more than once a week) _______
    2. Moderate (get inebriated once a week) _______
    3. Rarely (less than once a week) _______

    b. Smoking

    1. More than one pack a day _______
    2. About one pack a day _______
    3. Less than one pack a day _______
    4. Do not smoke _______

    c. Drugs (exclusive of medication)

    1. Indicate kind and method of taking _______________ (Kind)

       ___ Oral ___ Intravenous ___ Other, describe

       Intake ___ every day ___ once every few days ___ once per week ___ once every two weeks

       ___ once a month ___ once every few months

    2. None _______

    d. Exercise ___ great deal ___ moderate ___ mild ___ never

    e. Fatty foods ___ great deal ___ moderate ___ small amount ___ never

18. How do you feel about the doctor examining you: ___ good ___ doesn't bother me ___ resist it

19. Are you satisfied with the treatment you are getting? ___ yes ___ no

    Comment: ____

    ____

HEART DISEASE QUESTIONNAIRE - 5

20. Are your symptoms increased

	Yes	No	If yes, when
a. When you are emotionally upset?	____	____	__________
b. When you exercise?	____	____	__________
c. Under certain weather conditions?	____	____	__________
d. At certain seasons?	____	____	__________

e. Other times—Specify ____

____

APPENDIX C

HEADACHE QUESTIONNAIRE

(To be administered by Psychologist. Not to be administered by patient directly.)

____
Diagnosis

____
Medication

Name	Address	Telephone	Age

Marital Status ____ M __ S __ W __ D __ Anyone else in family have headaches? ________

Date First Notice Headaches ________ What were they? ________

<u>At That Time</u>

a. Anything unusual happening psychologically such as:

1. Mental stress or upset emotionally due to:

   a. Loss of someone close to you? _____ If so, what relation? ______
   b. Difficulty with career or money? _____
   c. Other? ____________________

To what extent do you think you are disabled:

1. Severely Disabled ____ 2. Moderately Disabled ____ 3. Not Disabled ____

What is the reaction of your relatives, friends, or acquaintances to your headaches?

	Indifferent	Greatly Upset	Moderately Upset	Mildly Upset	Other
Relatives	____	____	____	____	____
Friends	____	____	____	____	____
Acquaintances	____	____	____	____	____

Have you lost anyone (by death, moving, etc.) close to you before or after symptoms?

Father	Mother	Other Blood Relative	Other Person (Relationship)	None

If so, what were the changes in the symptoms? ________________

HEADACHE QUESTIONNAIRE - 2

As a child or adult, did you or do you have: (Please circle appropriate number)

1. Very often (Every Day)
2. Quite Often (Once every three days)
3. Moderately Often (Between one a week and one a month)
4. Hardly ever (Once or less)
5. Never

	Child	Adult
Headaches	1 2 3 4 5	1 2 3 4 5
Tremors	1 2 3 4 5	1 2 3 4 5
Tics	1 2 3 4 5	1 2 3 4 5
Convulsions	1 2 3 4 5	1 2 3 4 5
Enuresis (Bedwetting after 4 years of age)	1 2 3 4 5	1 2 3 4 5
Temper Tantrums	1 2 3 4 5	1 2 3 4 5
Stuttering	1 2 3 4 5	1 2 3 4 5
Heart Pains	1 2 3 4 5	1 2 3 4 5
Bite Nails	1 2 3 4 5	1 2 3 4 5
Suck Thumb	1 2 3 4 5	1 2 3 4 5

Do you get angry easily? ________ Yes ________ No

Do you withdraw from difficult situations? ________ Yes ________ No

If so, explain: ____________________

Comments ____________________

Do you consider yourself: Yes No

1. An ambitious person ___ ___
2. A persistent person ___ ___
3. Have good control of yourself ___ ___
4. A moody person ___ ___
   If yes, explain when you have change in moods ____________________
5. A clean person ___ ___
6. A dependent independent adequate inadequate person? (circle)
7. Are you able to express your feelings adequately or do you repress them?
   Expression of: Grief ______ Able ______ Unable   Joy ______ Able ______ Unable
   Rage ______ Able ______ Unable   Other emotions ______ Able ______ Unable
8. Do you conform most of the time to everyday mores? ______ Yes ______ No

HEADACHE QUESTIONNAIRE - 3

9. Do you dream at all? ________

   Frequency: Practically every night ____ Once every few nights ____
   One night per week ____ Less than one night per week ____

   Vividness: Very clear ____ Moderately Clear ____ Jumbled Up ____

   Duration: All night ____ Half the night ____ Less than 1/2 night ____

   What about? ____

10. Do you daydream? ________

    Frequency: Practically every day ____ Once every few days ____
    One day per week ____ Less than one day per week ____

    Vividness: Very Clear ____ Moderately Clear ____ Jumbled Up ____

    What about? ____

11. In relation to your family, describe:

    a. Mother's personality and how you got along with her ______________
    b. Father's personality and how you got along with him ______________
    c. Sibling's personality and how you got along with them ______________
    ____

12. In your home when you were growing up:

    a. Who was disciplinarian: ____ (Father) ____ (Mother) ______________ (Other person, relationship)

13. What is the feeling in your family about headaches? ______________

14. Do you or did any members of your family have any psychosomatic ailments, that is, sicknesses which have no apparent physical cause? ______________

    If yes: ____ (Father) ____ (Mother) ______________ (Other blood relative, relationship)

15. Work History: Current employment or last job ______________

    How long? ________ Dates ______________

    Enjoy current work or last job? ________ How getting along with boss or got along with boss? ___ (good) ___ (fair) ___ (badly) Other employees ___ (good) ___ (fair) ___ (badly)

    Past work ______________ (Type) ___ (None)

    How got along with boss ___ (good) ___ (fair) ___ (badly) Other employees ___ (good) ___ (fair) ___ (badly)

HEADACHE QUESTIONNAIRE - 4

16. Have you strong religious beliefs?

    1. Extremely religious (go to place of worship regularly and observe all religious holidays) ______
    2. Moderately religious (go to place of worship occasionally and observe some holidays) ______
    3. Rarely go to place of worship ______
    4. Never go to place of worship and never observe holidays ______

17. How much did/do you indulge in the following previous to having headaches?

    a. Alcohol

    1. Great deal (get inebriated more than once a week) ______
    2. Heavy (2–3 drinks every day) ______
    3. Moderate (one drink every day or 2–3 drinks or more on weekends) ______
    4. Light (occasionally, sometimes to inebriation) ______
    5. Rarely (occasionally, but never to inebriation) ______
    6. Never ______

    b. Smoking

    1. More than one pack a day ______
    2. About one pack a day ______
    3. Less than one pack a day ______
    4. Don't smoke ______

    c. Drugs (exclusive of medication)

    1. Indicate kind and method of taking ____________________ Kind

       ___ Oral ______ Intravenous ______ Other, describe

       Intake ______ every day ______ once every few days ______ once per week ______ once every two weeks ______ once a month ______ once every few months

    2. None ______

18. How do you feel about the doctor examining you: ___ good ______ doesn't bother me ___ resist it

19. Are you satisfied with the treatment you are getting? __ yes __ no

HEADACHE QUESTIONNAIRE - 5

20. Are your symptoms increased:

	Yes	No	If yes, when
a. When you are emotionally upset?	____	____	________
b. When you exercise?	____	____	________
c. Under certain weather conditions?	____	____	________
d. At certain seasons?	____	____	________

e. Other times? Specify ____

____

GROUP RESEARCH - RHEUMATOIDS

Category	*Rheumatoid Arthritics Rank*	*Controls Rank*
#1	4	2
#2	1	1
#3	5	3
#4	6	4
#5	10	9
#6	3	5
#7	2	6
#8	7	7
#9	8	8
#10	9	10
	N-22	N-22

Rheumatoids Rank Order

PROFILE SCORE MEANS AND PERCENTILES OF MIGRAINE PATIENTS

Test	*Mean Score*	*Percentile*
Cornell Index	15.08	13
Multiple Affect Check List		
Anxiety	7.22	52
Depression	12.26	53
Hostility	6.57	48

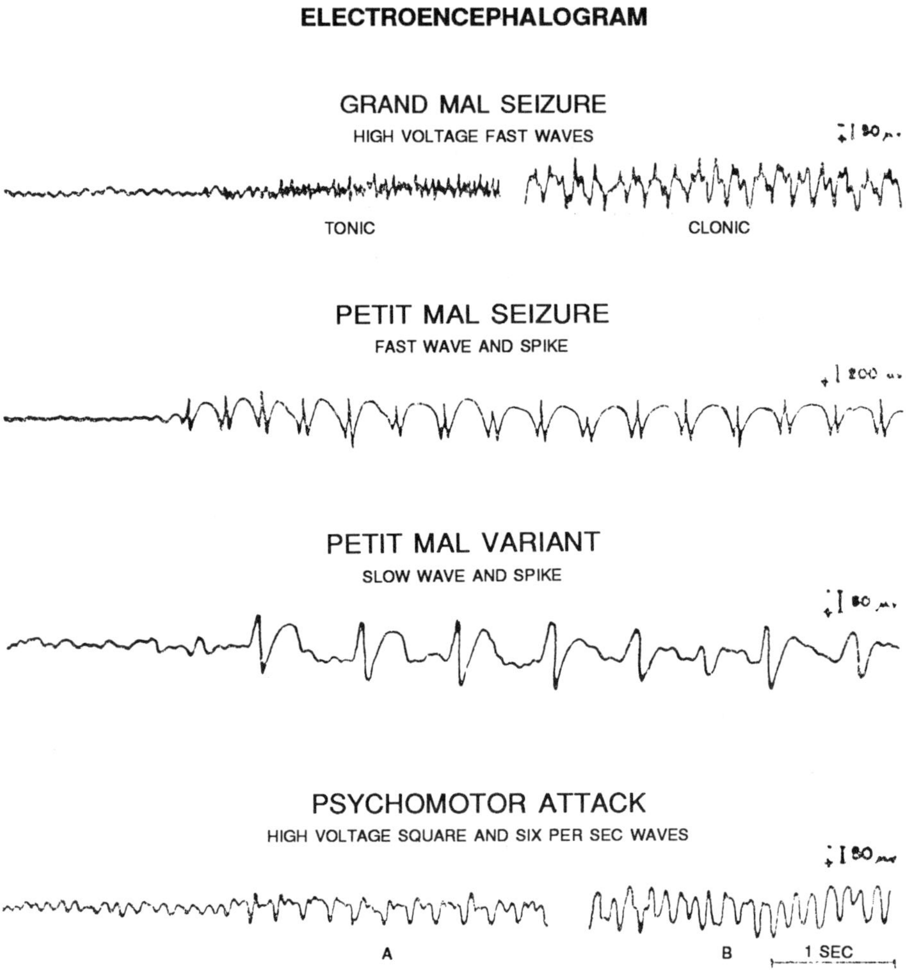

FIGURE II

Representative electroencephalograms of four patients to show records taken before, and during, four different types of seizures: grand mal, *two forms of* petit mal, *and psychic variant (psychomotor). At the right is the perpendicular deflection made by a 50-millionth or 200-millionth volt current, and at the bottom the time marked by one second. The left of each tracing is a portion of the person's normal record. The rest of the tracing was made during a seizure. Four different types of seizures are depicted:* (top to bottom) *(1) the tonic and, after an interval, the clonic phase of a* grand mal *convulsion; (2) the three-a-second alternate wave and spike of a* petit mal; *(3) the relatively slow rare (two-a-second) wave and spike called* Petit mal variant, *which is usually not accompanied by symptoms; (4) two phases of a psychomotor seizure.*
*See page 7.

BIBLIOGRAPHY

1. Alstrom, Carl Henry: A Study of Epilepsy in Its Clinical, Social and Genetic Aspects. Psychiatrie et Neurologica Supplementum, 63: Ejnib, Munksgaard Norregorde (Copenhagen 1952).
2. Arlow S: Identification Mechanisms in Coronary Occlusion. Psychosom Med 7, 1945, 95.
3. Bennett AL: The Personality of Rheumatoid Arthritis Patients A Study of 80 Rheumatoid Arthritis Patients from Clinics of 3 Mental Hospitals. Unpublished M.A. Thesis McGill U. 1952.
4. Bickerstaff ER: Basilar Artery Migraine, Lancet, 1:15, 1961.
5. Blum GE and Nichols G: Emotional Factors in Children with Rheumatoid Arthritis. Am J Orthopsychiatry, 24, 588, 1954.
6. Boland EW: Psychogenic Rheumatism: the Musculo-Skeletal Expression of Psychoneurosis. Calif Med 68, 273, 1948.
7. Bravais LF: Recherches sur Les Symptomes et le Traitement de le Epilepsie Hemiplegique. Thesis, Faculte of Medicine Paris 1827.
8. Breuer M, and Freud S: Studies in Hysteria, N.Y. Basic Books, 1957, 181.
9. Camfield Peter R, Metrakos Katherine and Andermann Frederick: Basilar Migraine, Seizures and Severe Epileptiform EEG Abnormalities Neurology Vol. 28, (6) 548–588, June 1978.
10. Chang A, Schalkwisk J, Happle R, Van de Kerkhof PC: Elastase-inhibiting Activity in Scaling Skin Disorders. Acto-Dermato-Venereolicha 1990, 70 (2) 147–151.
11. Cleveland SE and Fisher S: A comparison of Psychological Characteristics and Physiological Activity in Ulcer and Rheumatoid Arthritis, Group I Psychological Measures. Psychosom Med 22, 283, 1960.
12. ______. Behavior and Unconscious Fantasies of Patients with Rheumatoid Arthritis. Psychosom Med 16, 327, 1954.
13. ______. Body Image and Personality, Princeton, N.J., Van Nostrand Co. 1958.
14. Cohen EL: Brit J Derm and Syph 57, 1945, 135.
15. Critchely M: Prognosis in Migraine. Lancet, 1936, 2, 35.
16. Dunbar F: Psychosomatic Medicine, New York, Hoeber, 1943.
17. Engel GL, Hamburger WW, Reiser M, Plunkett J: Elentroencephalographic and Psychological Studies of a Case of Migraine with Severe Pre Headache Phenomena with Comments on Cerebral Vasospasm and Focal Hypertensive Encephalopathy. Psychosom Med 15, 1953, 337–148.
18. Engelman R: M.F. 8th Med J 34, 1079, 1941.
19. Felton BS, Revenson TA: Age Differences in Coping with Chronic Illness. Psychology and Aging. June 1987, 2(2) 164–170.
20. Ferrier D: Experimental Research in Cerebral Psychology and Pathology. West Lunatic Asylum, Medical Reports 3, 30–96, 1873.
21. Forssman O and Lindegord B: The Post Coronary Patient. A Multidisciplinary Investigation of Aged Swedish Males. J Psychosom Med 3, 1958, 9.

22. Freud Sigmund: Dostujewski und die Vatertotung: Gesammelte Schriften Vol. 12, Vienna, Internationaler Psychoanalytischen Verlag 1934.
23. ______. Collected Papers, Volume N.Y. International Psychoanalytic Press, 1924.
24. ______. Collected Papers, Vol. 1, International University Press, N.Y., 1924, 76.
25. Friedman M and Rosenman RH: Overt Behavior in Coronary Artery Disease with Blood and Cardiovascular Findings. JAMA 189, 1964, 1286.
26. ______. A Comparison of Fat Intake of American Men and Women, Possible Relationship to Incidence of Clinical Coronary Heart Disease. Report #24 from Laboratory of Clinical Stress Research, Stockholm, Nov. 1971.
27. Fritsch G and Hitzig E: "Über die Elektrische Wissensch. Erregbarkeit des Grosshirns. Arch Anat Physiol, U Wissench. Med 1950, 37, 300–332, 1870.
28. Gascon G and Harlow C: Juvenile Migraine; Presenting an Acute Confusional State, Pediatrics, 45, 635–682, 1970.
29. Geist H: Psychological Aspects of Rheumatoid Arthritis, Springfield, C. C. Thomas, 1964.
30. Gentry WD, Foster S and Haney T: Denial as a Determinent of Anxiety and Perceived Health Status in a Coronary Care Unit. Psychosom Medicine, 34, 1, Jan–Feb 1972, 39–94.
31. Gibbs FA and Gibbs EL: Atlas of Electroencephalography. Cambridge, Cummings 1941.
32. Ginsparb SL and Satten S: Psychiatric Aspects of Rehabilitation in Coronary Artery Disease. Proceedings of the 78 Annual Convention of the American Psychological Association, 1970.
33. Goldstein H: What are Diffuse Neurodermatitis and Atopic Dermatitis. Vestnik Dermatologii Venerolog II, 1989, 31-34.
34. Goodell H, Lowontin R and Wolff H: The Familial Occurrence of a Migraine Headache, a Study of Heredity. Ass Research Nerv and Ment Dis 1954, 33, 346.
35. Gowers WR: Epilepsy and Other Chronic Convulsive Diseases: Their Causes, Symptoms and Treatment. New York, Dover Publications 1964.
36. Graham JR: The Natural History of Migraine: Some Observations and a Hypothesis. Trans Amer Clin, and Climat Assoc 1952, 64, 61.
37. Greenhill J and Finesinger M: Arch Dermat and Syph 46, 187, 1942.
38. Gressel GC, Shobe FO, Saslow G, Duboism PM, Schroeder HA: Personality Factors in Arterial Hypertension JAMA 1949, 140, 265–272.
39. Grimes E: The Migraine Instability, M. J. and Rec 1931, 134, 417.
40. Halliday JL: Psychosomatic Medicine and the Rheumatism Problem, Practitioner, 152, 6, 1944.
41. ______. Psychological Aspects of Rheumatoid Arthritis, Proc Royal Soc Medicine, 35, 455, 1942.
42. Hench FS, Finney JA, Boland EW: Precipitin and Predisposing Factors in Rheumatoid Arthritis, Ann Rheum Dis 6, 91, 1947.
43. Herzer H, Herzer R, Rebeuding G, Altenstein R, Brimberger J: Structural

Differentiation of Psychological Performance in Epilepsy. Psychiatrie, Neurologie und Medizinische Psychologie, 1987, June 39, (6), 321–39.
44. Heyden S: Unpublished data.
45. Hickam JB, Cargill WH and Golden A: Cardiovascular Reactions to Emotional Stimuli Effect on the Cardiac Output; Arteriovenous Oxygen Difference, Arterial Pressure and Peripheral Resistance. J Clinical Investigation, 27, 1948, 290.
46. Hinkle A, et al: Occupation, Education and Coronary Heart Disease, Science, 161, 1968, 238–245.
47. Hodgson GA: Brit J Derm and Syph 57, 1945, 125.
48. Holubar K: History of Psoriasis and Parapsoriasis Gesnerus, 1989, 46, PC, 34:257–63.
49. Ibrahim MA, et al: Personality Traits and Coronary Utilization of a Cross Sectional Study Devised to Test Whether a Psychological Profile Precedes or Follows Manifest Coronary Disease. J Chronic Dis 19, 1966, 255–271.
50. Jackson J Hughlings: On Epilepsy and Epileptiform Convulsions, in James Taylor (Ed.,) Selected Writing of J Hughling Jackson (vol. 1), London, Hodder and Stoughton 1931.
51. Jellife SW and Evans E: New York Med J 104, 177, 1916.
52. Jick H and Slone D, et al: Boston Collaborative Drug Surveillance Program, Lancet II, 1972, 1271–1278.
53. ______. Coffee and Mycardial Infarction. New England Journal of Medicine 89, 1973, 37–63.
54. Jokiel R, Tammen AT, Jerre M, Lonory F, Blumchen G: Personality Psychological Correlates of Blood Pressure Behavior. Group Comparison of Hypertensive and Normative Heart Patients. Correlates of Blood Pressure. Herz, 1987, April 12 (2) 141–145.
55. Kalamkarian AA, Samsov VA, Rukisanikova JH: Methods of Treatment in Dermatoses. Sovietskaia Meditsina, 1989 (8) 27–31.
56. Kasanin A, et al: The Significance of Psychic and Socio-Economic Stress and other Modes of Life in the Etiology of Myocardial Infarction. Annals Med Interal Fenn, Suppl 43, 1963, 52.
57. Kemple C: Rorschach Method and Psychosomatic Personality Traits of Patients with Rheumatic Disease, Hypertensive Vascular Disease, Coronary Occlusion and Fracture. Psychosomatic Med 7, 1945, 85–89.
58. Kent A, Drummond LM: Acne Excorie—A Case Report on Treatment Using Habit Reversal. Clinical and Experimental Dermatology, 1989, March 14(2) 163–164.
59. Kugoh T, Fukonish I, Kosokanah K, Kashiharak Jora I: Psychological Aspects of Families with Epileptic Patients. A Study Using a General Health Questionnaire. Japanese Journal of Psychiatry and Neurology, 1989, Sept. 43(3) 550–1.
60. Laihiner A: Psychosomatic Aspects in Dermatoses. Ann Clin Res 1987, 19(2) 147–149.
61. Lambert VA, Lambert CE Jr: Coping with Rheumatoid Arthritis. Nursing Clinics of N. America, 1987, Sept. 22(3) 551–558.

62. Lambert VA: Study of Factors Associated with Psychological Well Being in Rheumatoid Arthritic Women. Image J Nurs, Sch 1985 17:50–53, 1985.
63. Lawall John and Domman D, Kilpatrick J: Basilar Artery Migraine. Journal of Nervous and Mental Diseases. Vol. 166, (11), 809–811, November 1978.
64. Lennox WG: Mental Defect in Epilepsy and the Influence of Heredity. Am J Psychiatry, 98, 733–39, 1942.
65. ______. Science and Seizures, New York, Harper and Brothers, 1941.
66. Lipskii LI, Katzaneiskll VK, Gmyzin SM: Treatment of Patients with Phlogmons of the Hand. Khirvrgiia, 1987, ct. (10) 24–27.
67. Ludwig AO: Psychogenic Factors in Rheumatoid Arthritis; Their Bearing on the Care and Rehabilitation of the Patient Psychother Rev 29, 339, 1949.
68. Maeland JG, Marik OE: After the Myocardial Infarction. A Medical and Psychological Study with Special Emphasis on Perceived Ideas. Scandinavian J of Rehabilitation Med Suppl 1989, 22, 1–87.
69. Marty R, de Muizan J, David CL: Investigation Psychosomatique Presses Universitaires, Paris, 1965.
70. Master DR, Thompson C, Dunn G, Lishman WA: Memory Selectivity and Unilateral Cerebral Dysfunction. Psychoanalitical Medicine, 1986, No. 16(4), 781–788.
71. Miles HW, Waldfogel S, Barrabbee EL, Cobb S: Psychosomatic Med 16, 1954, 455–477.
72. Moldofsky H, Chester WS: Pain and Mood Patterns in Patients with Rheumatoid Arthritis. Psychosomatic Medicine 32, 309, 1970.
73. Moos Rudolph A: Social Ecological Perspective on Medical Disorders in Wittkower, Eric D and Warner, Hector. Psychosom Med. Its Clinical Applications, Harper and Rowe, Hagerstown, Md., 1977, 199–204.
74. Nattero G, Delorenzo C, Biale L, Allais G, Torre E, Ancone M: Psychological Aspect of Weekend Headache Sufferers in Comparison with Migraine Patients. Headache, 1989, Feb. 29 (2) 93–99.
75. ______. Menstrual Migraine; New Biological and Psychological Aspects, Headache, 1989, March 28(1) 103–107.
76. Negro FE, Rinaldi R, Lolli D: Psychological Aspects of People with Headaches Undergoing Percutaneous Electro Stimulation Preliminary Data. Am Journal Chinese Medicine 1989, 16 (1–2); 71–74.
77. Nemiah JC and Sifneos PE: Affect and Fantasy in Patients with Psychosomatic Disorders in Hill, O.W. Modern Trends in Psychosomatic Medicine, London, Butterworth, 1970.
78. Nikitina P: Effect of the Health Status of Parents and Family Life Style on the Occurence of Allergy Dermatoses. Pediatrii, 1988 (5) 59–61.
79. Parkes CM, et al: Broken Heart: A Statistical Study of Increased Mortality Among Widowers. Med J, 1, 1969, 740.
80. Pateli C, Halmot HG: Stress Management, Blood Pressure and Quality of Life. Journal of Hypertension Supplement 1987, 5 (1) 521–28.
81. Paul O: Stimulants and Coronaries, Postgraduate Medicine, 44, 1968, 96–199.
82. Petzold R, Bergman G: Anxiety, The Heart Patient and Organization of

Psychosomatic Medicine Schweizishe Rundscharfür Medizin Praxis 1989, No. 78. 46, 1288–92.

83. Pieper C, Lacroix AZ, Kaeasek RA: The Relation of Psychosocial Dimensions of Work with Coronary Heart Disease Risk Factors. A Meta Analysis of 5 U.S. Data Bases. Am J Epidemiology, 1989, May 29 (1) 483–494.
84. Rahe RH and Passikivi J: Psychosocial Factors and Myocardial Infarction. J Psychosomatic Research, 15, 1971, 33.
85. Ramsay R Alec: Psychiatric Considerations in Chronic Pain, in Wittkower Eric. D. and Warner, Hector. Psychosomatic Medicine Its Clinical Applications, Harper and Rowe, Hagerstown, Md., 1977, 57–63.
86. Rennie TA: The Role of Personality in Certain Hypertensive States, New England Journal of Medicine, 221, 1939, 448–456.
87. Rosenman RH, et al: A Predictive Study of Coronary Heart Disease, JAMA 189, 1964, 15–22.
88. Sacks Oliver: Migraine, the Evolution of A Common Disease. Berkeley, University of California Press, 1970.
89. Saul LJ: Emotional Maturity, The Development and Dynamics of Personality. J. P. Lippincott, Phil. Pa., 1947.
90. Samsonov VA, Zhukivai K: Comparative Analysis of the Clinical Effectiveness of Reflexotherapy and Psychopharmaco Therapy in the Treatment of Neurotic Disorders in Dermatology Patients. Vestnick de Toplogii Venerologii, 1979 (7), 34–37.
91. Shekell RB, Ostfeld AM, Paul O: Social Status and Incidence of Coronary Heart Disease. J Chron Dis 22, 1969, 381–394.
92. Stevenson IP, Duncan CH: Ripley-Variations in the Electrocardiogram with Changes in the Emotional State Geriatrics, 6, 1953, 164.
93. Stine LA: Brief Psychotherapy of Psychiatric Reactions to Physical Illness, the Medical Patients in the Psychology of Medical Practice, Marc H. Hollender, Editor, W. B. Saunders 1958, 36–39.
94. Stokes JH: Arch Derm Syph 22, 803, 1930.
95. Syme SL, et al: Some Social and Cultural Factors Associated with Occurrence of Coronary Heart Disease, J Chronic Dis 17, 1964, 272–289.
96. Teiger William: Some Aspects of Psychogenic Rheumatism. Rheum Dis 105, 1952.
97. Toor M, Katsensky A, Agmon J, Alkalou F: Arteriosclerosis and Related Factors in Immigrants in Israel, Circulation, 22, 1960, 265–279.
98. Van der Valk JM and Groen JS: Personality Structure and Conflict Situation in Patients with Myocardial Infarction. J Psychosomatic Research, 11, 1967, 41.
99. Wahlberg JD: Occupational Atopic Dermatitis. Lakartidhingen, 1989, March 1, 86 (9) 703.
100. Wardwell WI, Hyman M, Bahnson CB: Socioeconomic Antecedants to Coronary Heart Disease in 87 White Males. Social Science and Med 2, 1968, 165.
101. Weiss E: Psychogenic Rheumatism. Arch Int Med 26, 1947.

102. Weiss E, Olin R, Rollin HH, Fisher HR and Bepler D: Emotional Factors in Coronary Occlusion, AMA Arch Inter Med 99, 1957, 628–641.
103. Wendkos MS: The influence of Autonomic Imbalance on the Human Electrocardiogram, American Heart Journal, 28, 1944, 549.
104. Wilhelmn L and Tribben R: Unpublished study.
105. Wittkower Eric, Russell Brian: Emotional Factors in Skin Disease, Paul B. Hoeber Inc., New York, 1953.
106. Wolff GA Jr and Wolff HG: Studies on the Nature of Certain Symptoms Associated with Cardiovascular Disorders, Psychosom Med 8, 1946, 239–319.
107. Wolff HG: Headache and Other Head Pain. New York, Oxford University Press, 1948.
108. Yakovlev Paul I and Hoskins Morgan. A Study of Neurosomatic Deterioration in Epilepsy. Assoc Res Nerv Ment Dis 1931, Part II.

AUTHOR INDEX

Y

SUBJECT INDEX